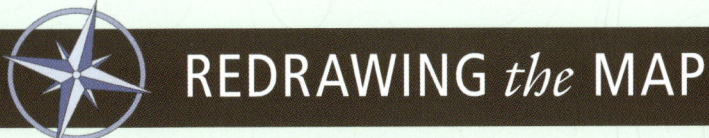

The Partition of India

KATE SHOUP

New York

Published in 2019 by Cavendish Square Publishing, LLC
243 5th Avenue, Suite 136, New York, NY 10016

Copyright © 2019 by Cavendish Square Publishing, LLC

First Edition

No part of this publication may be reproduced, stored in a retrieval system, or transmitted in any form or by any means—electronic, mechanical, photocopying, recording, or otherwise—without the prior permission of the copyright owner. Request for permission should be addressed to Permissions, Cavendish Square Publishing, 243 5th Avenue, Suite 136, New York, NY 10016. Tel (877) 980-4450; fax (877) 980-4454.

Website: cavendishsq.com

This publication represents the opinions and views of the author based on his or her personal experience, knowledge, and research. The information in this book serves as a general guide only. The author and publisher have used their best efforts in preparing this book and disclaim liability rising directly or indirectly from the use and application of this book.

All websites were available and accurate when this book was sent to press.

Library of Congress Cataloging-in-Publication Data

Names: Shoup, Kate, 1972- author.
Title: The Partition of India / Kate Shoup.
Description: First edition. | New York : Cavendish Square, 2019. | Series: Redrawing the Map | Includes bibliographical references and index.
Identifiers: LCCN 2017058835 (print) | LCCN 2017060337 (ebook) | ISBN 9781502635600 (eBook) | ISBN 9781502635594 (library bound) | ISBN 9781502635617 (pbk.)
Subjects: LCSH: India—History--Partition, 1947-—Juvenile literature. | India—History—British occupation, 1765-1947. | India--History--Autonomy and independence movements—Juvenile literature. | India—History—1947-—Juvenile literature.
Classification: LCC DS480.842 (ebook) | LCC DS480.842 .S483 2019 (print) | DDC 954.03/59—dc23
LC record available at https://lccn.loc.gov/2017058835

Editorial Director: David McNamara
Editor: Erin L. McCoy
Copy Editor: Michele Suchomel-Casey
Associate Art Director: Amy Greenan
Designer: Jessica Nevins
Production Coordinator: Karol Szymczuk
Photo Research: J8 Media

The photographs in this book are used by permission and through the courtesy of: Cover, Luciano Mortula/Alamy Stock; p. 5 SelfQ, own work/File: Dominion of Pakistan & Indian Controlled Kashmir).svg (orthographic projection/Wikimedia Commons; p. 6 User: The_Red_Hat_of_Pat_Ferrick/File: The British Empire Anachronous.png/Wikimedia Commons; p. 9 STR/AFP/Getty Images; p. 11 Avantiputra7, own work/File: Indus Valley Civilization, Mature Phase (2600-1900 Download BCE).png/Wikimedia Commons; p. 15 Marzolino/Shutterstock.com; p. 16 Alexander Bassano (1829-1913) Scanned from the book The National Portrait Gallery History of the Kings and Queens of England by David Williamson, ISBN 1855142287, p. 153/File: Queen Victoria by Bassano.jpg/Wikimedia Commons; p. 19 Unknown/ http://www.movinghere.org.uk/galleries/histories/asian/origins/origins.htm#relationship Moving Here - Heritage. Originally uploaded on English Wikipedia by Fowler & fowler (talk) A. O. Hume, the founder of the Indian National Congress, is shown in the middle (third row from the front). To his right is Dadabhoy Nairoji; to his left, in sequence, are: W. C. Bonnerjee, Pherozeshah Mehta, and Gopal Krishna Gokhale/File: 1st INC1885.jpg/Wikimedia Commons; pp. 20-21 Chronicle/Alamy Stock Photo; pp. 26-27 Dinodia Photos/Alamy Stock Photo; p. 28 The Print Collector/Getty Images; p. 32-33, 60 Keystone-France/Gamma-Keystone/Getty Images; p. 37 Photograph by Amrita Shergil, reproduced in Tony Halliday, ed. (1992) Insight Guides: Pakistan. Published by Apa Publications (HK) Ltd.)/File: Iqbal 140x190.jpg/Wikimedia Commons; p. 41 Photographer not known/Published in Muhammad Ali Jinnah: A Political Study by Matlubul Hassan Saiyid (Lahore: Shaikh Muhammad Ashraf, 1945), plate following page 807. Copyright expired 1995/File: Jinnah and Gandhi.jpg/Wikimedia Commons; p. 45 SSPL/Getty Images; p. 46 Sgt. A Stubbs/IWM via Getty Images; p. 48 Universal History Archive/UIG/Getty Images; p. 51 Keystone/Hulton Archive/Getty Images; p. 56 © Hulton-Deutsch Collection/Corbis/Getty Images; p. 62 Universal History Archive/Getty Images; p. 63 Furfur/This file was derived from: Pakistan Ost- und West 1971.svg/File: Pakistan Ost- und West 1971 (2).svg/Wikimedia Commons; p. 64 Dinodia Photos/Getty Images; p. 66 The Hindustan Times/File: The Hindustan Times front page 15 August 1947 (1187 × 1600).jpg/Wikimedia Commons; p. 69 Edward Miller/Keystone/Hulton Archive/Getty Images; p. 73 Nicolas Merky, own work/File: Indo-Bangladeshi Barrier.JPG/Wikimedia Commons; p. 75 Khan Ahmed Raza, own work/File: Punjab-religion-2.jpg/Wikimedia Commons; p. 78 World History Archive/Alamy Stock Photo; p. 81 Own work/File: Partition of India 1947 en.svg/Wikimedia Commons; p. 83 STRINGER/AFP/Getty Images; pp. 86-87 Bettmann/Getty Images; p. 89 Margaret Bourke-White/The LIFE Picture Collection/Getty Images; p.91 Buyenlarge/Getty Images; p. 96 Arif Ali/AFP/Getty Images.

Printed in the United States of America

CONTENTS

Chapter 1	**Empire, Independence, and Partition**	**4**
Chapter 2	**The Long Road to Indian Independence**	**10**
Chapter 3	**Partition**	**36**
Chapter 4	**The Radcliffe Line**	**65**
Chapter 5	**The Fallout**	**80**

Chronology   **97**

Glossary   **101**

Further Information   **103**

Bibliography   **105**

Index   **109**

About the Author   **112**

CHAPTER ONE
Empire, Independence, and Partition

Beginning in the sixteenth century CE, Great Britain embarked on a series of conquests. It acquired land all over the globe to establish important and lucrative networks for trade. By 1913, the British Empire, as it was known, had hundreds of millions of people within its purview. By 1921, at its territorial peak, the empire's dominion, colonies, protectorates, and other territories covered almost 14 million square miles (more than 35 million square kilometers)—nearly one-quarter of all land on the planet.

Without question, the "jewel in the crown" of the British Empire was the Indian subcontinent in South Asia, which Great Britain acquired in 1757. India was valuable for several reasons. First, it was rich in natural resources and agricultural products. These proved vital to British industry and trade. Second, it had large

The Indian subcontinent comprises modern-day India (*shown above in yellow*) and Pakistan (*shown in dark green*), along with Bangladesh, Bhutan, Maldives, Nepal, and Sri Lanka. Kashmir, a disputed territory to which India, Pakistan, and China all lay claim, is shown in light green.

numbers of skilled laborers working for low wages. Third, it was perfectly situated to control the flow of trade between Europe and the East. And fourth, it represented an enormous market for British goods. Not surprisingly, Britain was reluctant to give India up.

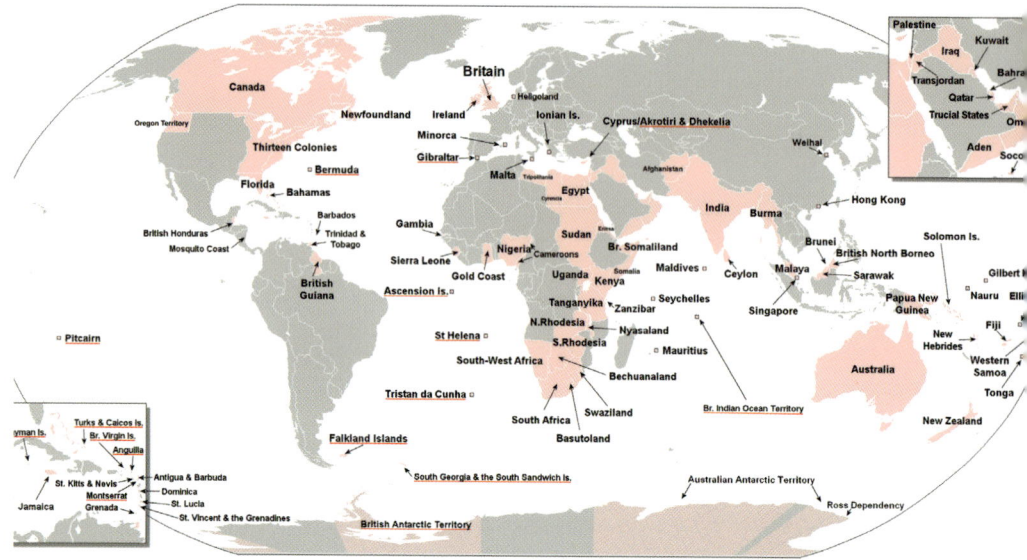

At its peak, the British Empire spanned the globe, covering more than 14 million square miles (35 million sq km).

In the aftermath of World War II (1939–1945), Great Britain faced a painful predicament. Exhausted by a war that had emptied its coffers and resulted in the deaths of more than four hundred thousand British soldiers and civilians, it could no longer absorb the costs associated with its empire, and that included India. It had no choice but to grant the region independence, which many of its residents had long desired.

Britain did not simply surrender its claim over India. It also split the country in two. This gave Muslim Indians a homeland, called Pakistan, while leaving the rest of India primarily in the care of its Hindu population. This split was called partition. Sadly, partition—or, more accurately, the manner in which it was carried out—proved disastrous.

A Flawed Strategy

What Britain *should* have done, some historians argue, was follow a precise set of steps over a period of multiple years. First, it should have disentangled soldiers from the British Indian Army to form the new Indian Army and Pakistani Armed Forces. Then, these forces should have been deployed in areas where the border between the two countries would likely fall. Then, and only then, should British officials have announced the exact placement of the boundary and commenced with partition.

As it happened, partition did not follow this sequence. Indeed, notes historian Andrew Roberts, these events happened "in almost the reverse order," over a period of just seventy-three days. The consequences, says Roberts, were "horrific." Due to widespread sectarian violence, millions of Indians were displaced from their homes and as many as two million died.

To be fair, even the order of events put forth by Roberts might not have ensured the peaceful partition of India. This is because Hindus, Muslims, and other populations in India were—in the words of a British civil service officer named Malcolm Darling—"as mixed up as the ingredients of a well-made pilau." This made it virtually impossible to draw a border that satisfied all parties. Still, as one British official in India observed, "I

Empire, Independence, and Partition 7

MASS MIGRATION
In the many months before and after partition, an estimated twelve million people crossed the border between Pakistan and India—among the largest mass migrations in history.

am sure that if [the border region] had been given time (say eight or nine months) to sort out their services properly, the terrible massacres of August-September-October would never have happened on anything approaching the scale that they did assume."

An Enduring Legacy

Historian Yasmin Khan describes 1947, the year of both independence and partition, as "a perfect storm of hope and disaster, leadership and blunder," observing that "not even a dozen people made momentous decisions affecting 400 million." It's no wonder, then, that more than seventy years later, the wounds of partition have not healed. Indeed, journalist William Dalrymple observes, "Partition is central to modern identity in the Indian subcontinent, ... branded painfully onto the regional consciousness by memories of almost unimaginable violence." Acclaimed Pakistani historian Ayesha Jalal agrees, calling partition "the central historical event in twentieth century South Asia."

Even today, partition colors relations between India and Pakistan, which remain hostile. Many analysts believe that an "uninterrupted and uninterruptible"

A building in Amritsar is in ruins following post-partition unrest in August 1947.

dialogue is the only means to achieve peace, while others argue that a number of other factors are at play. Regardless, peace remains elusive—and may remain so for some time.

CHAPTER TWO
The Long Road to Indian Independence

The Indian subcontinent has a long history of diverse peoples, religions, and advanced cultures living and working together. The territory would eventually come under British rule, a transition that would ultimately lead to the formation of the two countries we today call India and Pakistan.

Early Indian History

Early humans settled the Indus Valley—now home to Pakistan and northern India—more than sixty thousand years ago. By 3300 BCE, the descendants of these early settlers formed an advanced society called the Indus Valley Civilization (IVC). Among the earliest-known human civilizations, the IVC thrived for two

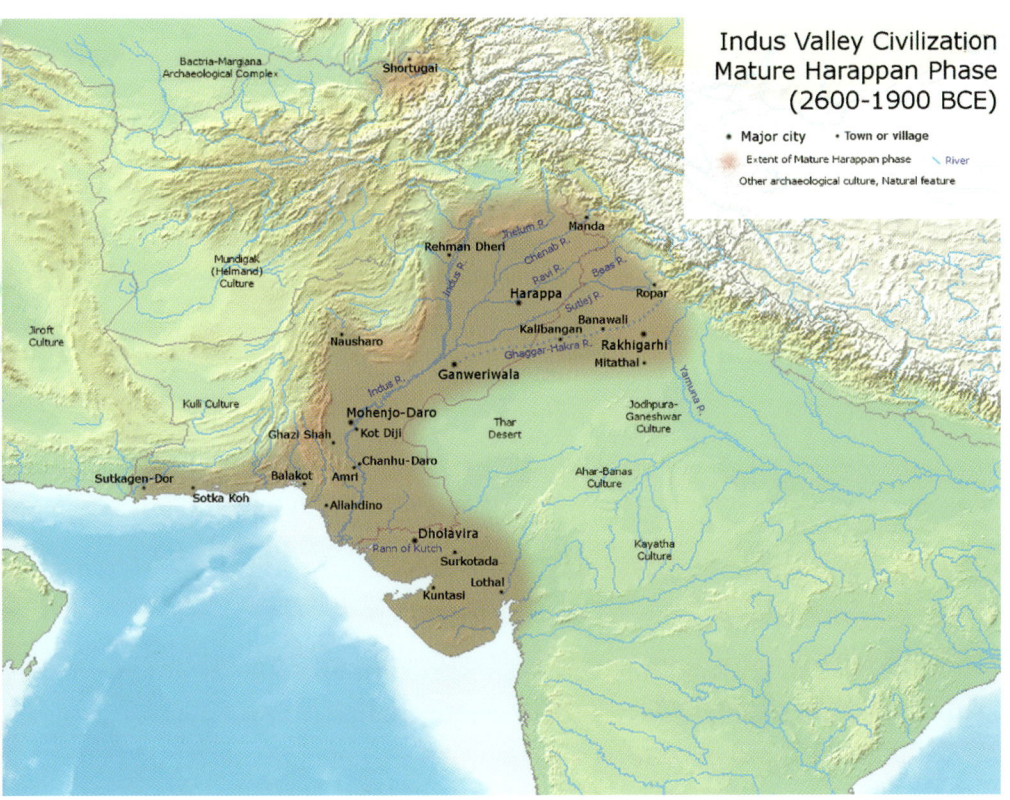

The Indus Valley Civilization was among the most advanced civilizations of its time.

millennia, boasting some five million inhabitants at its height. Most of these ancient people lived in cities—well-planned areas with clearly defined neighborhoods, massive protective walls, and sewer and drainage systems that were far superior to those found elsewhere in the world at that time. Indeed, these systems were more advanced than those used in many areas of

The Long Road to Indian Independence

Pakistan and India today. Homes in larger cities even had flush toilets.

Perhaps due to drought, the IVC suffered a slow decline beginning around 1300 BCE. The urban population scattered, spreading throughout the Indian subcontinent to settle in isolated farms and small villages. The subcontinent then broke into several kingdoms, sultanates, and republics, which rose and fell over time. One of these was the Delhi sultanate, an Islamic government founded in 1206 CE. Muslim rule continued under the Mughal Empire, which conquered the Delhi sultanate in 1526. Ultimately, the Mughal Empire spanned almost the entire Indian subcontinent and ruled some 150 million people.

Together, the Delhi sultanate and Mughal Empire mixed Hindu culture with Islamic traditions—a fusion that would endure for centuries. Indeed, the last Mughal emperor, crowned in 1837, noted that Hinduism and Islam "share[d] the same essence."

British Rule

By the mid-1700s, following a series of military defeats, the Mughal Empire had begun to contract. The East India Company, a British business founded in 1600 to pursue trade in South and Southeast Asia, hastened the empire's demise by purchasing vast tracts of land. In the late 1700s, the firm assumed governance over much of the Indian subcontinent, ushering in a period known as company rule.

In May 1857, provoked by the imposition of invasive social reforms and high taxes by the East India Company, thousands of Indians rebelled. Violence erupted in the town of Meerut and quickly spread to the cities of Delhi, Jhansi, Kanpur, Lucknow, and beyond. This rebellion ended in defeat in June 1858. However, it represented a turning point. Specifically, it prompted the passage of the Government of India Act 1858, which called for the liquidation of the East India Company and placed India under the direct rule of the British government.

Conscious of the conditions that had sparked the unrest, the British monarch, Queen Victoria, sought to quell concerns about British rule in India (often referred to as the British Raj). In November 1858, she issued a proclamation that granted Indians many important rights. The proclamation elevated the status of Indians to that of all other British subjects; called for religious freedom; ensured that all Indians would be entitled to work for the British Crown regardless of "Race or Creed"; and mandated that the law be framed and administered with "due regard ... to the ancient Rights, Usages, and Customs of India." The proclamation even went so far as to offer clemency to participants in the rebellion (except those convicted of murdering British subjects during the unrest), promising "unconditional Pardon, Amnesty, and Oblivion of all Offence against Ourselves, Our Crown and Dignity, on their return to their homes and peaceful pursuits."

THE DELHI SULTANATE

Before the tenth century, the Indian subcontinent resembled a patchwork of different Hindu and Buddhist kingdoms. Starting around 960 CE, Muslim armies from Central Asia began raiding many of these kingdoms—particularly those in the northern portion of the subcontinent. These constant attacks were disruptive but ultimately unsuccessful. That changed in 1173, when forces led by Sultan Mu'izz ad-Din Muhammad Ghori of the nearby Ghurid Empire successfully occupied the region.

Mu'izz ad-Din conquered northern India. But it was his successor who founded the Delhi sultanate in 1206. This first sultan of Delhi—a former *mamluk*, or "slave," named Qutb al-Din Aibak—consolidated control over northern India and spawned a powerful dynasty, called the Mamluk dynasty, that reigned until 1290.

Four more dynasties followed. First came the Khalji dynasty (1290–1320), during which the Delhi sultanate grew to encompass broader swathes of northwestern India. Next came the Tughlaq dynasty (1320–1414), which eventually occupied nearly all of the Indian subcontinent. It was also one of the few states in Asia to successfully repel attacks by the powerful Mongol Empire—although Mongols did successfully sack the city of Delhi in 1398.

The Delhi sultanate's borders contracted during the Sayyid dynasty (1414–1451). This occurred because of various factors, including Hindu rebellions, invasions by neighboring states, and the creation of new Muslim states within the sultanate's lands. By the end of the Lodi dynasty (1451–1526), the sultanate's territory was even smaller.

The sultanate became easy prey for a Central Asian leader named Babur. Babur—a descendant of two famous Mongol conquerors, Tamerlane and Genghis Khan—defeated the sultanate in 1526 to establish the Mughal Empire. The Delhi sultanate lasted just 320 years, but its impact on India remains. During the Delhi sultanate, the Indian subcontinent's economy and population blossomed. This period also saw the emergence of the Hindustani language, which incorporated elements of Sanskrit, Arabic, and Persian, and was the basis of both Hindi and Urdu—languages that are still spoken today.

Babur, descendant of the famous Mongol conquerer Genghis Khan, became the first emperor of the Mughal dynasty in 1525.

Queen Victoria reigned over the British Empire, including the Indian subcontinent, from 1837 to 1876.

The British Raj in the Early 1900s

By the advent of the twentieth century, the British government had organized India into eight large provinces, each controlled by a British governor or lieutenant governor. In addition to these were five minor provinces administered by chief commissioners. These officials answered to the British governor-general of India, also called the viceroy, who in turn reported to the British secretary of state for India (and, through him, the British Parliament), based in London. Advising the secretary of state in London was the Council of India, which initially consisted of fifteen Englishmen, each of whom had spent at least ten years on the Indian subcontinent, but would later include two Indian representatives.

The viceroy also worked with an executive council, or cabinet, in India. This body consisted of six appointed British members, each responsible for one area of governance: home, revenue, military, law, finance, or public works. For the passage of laws, this executive council was expanded into a legislative

PRINCELY STATES

The British Raj covered most of the Indian subcontinent—but not all of it. Sprinkled throughout were nearly six hundred princely states. These states—some as small as 10 square miles (25 sq km) in size—had varying degrees of independence under British rule.

council, which was eventually called the Imperial Legislative Council. It included as many as twelve additional appointed members. Half of these were British officials, and the other half—who served only in an advisory capacity—were Indians (usually members of the Indian aristocracy who were loyal to the Crown) or people from Great Britain who lived in India but did not work for the Crown. Similar localized legislative councils existed in each of the eight provinces.

Life in the British Raj

The British government in India imposed its own brand of order on the Indian subcontinent. It introduced a new penal code and updated civil and criminal legal procedures. It built an extensive bureaucracy to handle the registration of births, deaths, marriages, adoptions, property deeds, and wills. It constructed schools and established universities. It backed key infrastructure projects, such as roadways, bridges, railways, canals, ports, telegraph lines, and irrigation systems. It encouraged industrialization. Finally, it assembled a military. As a result of these measures, India's economy expanded and its middle class flourished.

As observed by economist Angus Maddison, the British government also "contributed to public health by introducing smallpox vaccination, establishing Western medicine and training modern doctors, … killing rats, and establishing quarantine procedures." As a result, "the death rate fell and the population of India grew by 1947 to more than two-and-a-half times its size in 1757."

A Desire for Autonomy

In some respects, the British Raj improved life in India. But in many important ways, it made life worse. For one thing, the country's population growth under the British Raj resulted in the overcrowding of cities and in regular and widespread famine, particularly among the poor. For another, Britain imposed crippling taxes to fund the extensive (and expensive) Indian bureaucracy and military. Perhaps worst of all, Britain—having retained for itself all economic power in India—

The Indian National Congress met for the first time in 1885. The Congress would become an important political body.

drained the country of its wealth by reinvesting the fruits of the Indian economy in England rather than in India.

Not surprisingly, many Indians longed for greater autonomy under British rule. To that end, a group of highly educated Indians—Hindus and Muslims alike—formed a political party called the Indian National Congress in 1885. The Congress's goal was to ensure educated Indians a larger role in government and build opportunities for them to engage in political and civic dialogue with the British Raj.

In this, the Congress was somewhat successful. The Indian Councils Act of 1892 increased the number of appointed Indian representatives in the provincial and national legislative councils. The Indian Councils Act of 1909—also called the Morley-Minto Reforms—went further. Among

Right: Lord George Curzon (*center, with gun*) served as viceroy of India from 1899 to 1905. Curzon implemented the partition of Bengal in 1905.

20 The Partition of India

The Long Road to Indian Independence   21

other things, these reforms increased the number of Indians permitted in government and allowed for their election rather than their appointment. Although the number of eligible voters was small, this reform resulted in a more representative government body—one loyal not only to Britain but also to India.

The Division of Bengal and a Growing Religious Divide

In 1905, the viceroy of India, Lord George Curzon, divided the Indian province of Bengal into two: West Bengal and East Bengal and Assam. West Bengal—home to the city of Calcutta and to thousands of factories and mills—retained a Hindu majority. East Bengal and Assam—rich in fertile farmland and natural resources—now had a Muslim majority. Lord Curzon insisted that this partition of Bengal would promote administrative efficiency. Much of the Indian citizenry, however, saw the partition of Bengal as a blatant attempt to "divide and rule," with religion as the divisor.

For centuries, Hindu and Muslim populations in India—not to mention Sikhs, Buddhists, Christians, and others—had peacefully coexisted. Indians simply did not differentiate themselves according to their religion. Instead, they divided themselves by class. In the words of journalist William Dalrymple, "A Sunni weaver from Bengal would have had far more in common in his language, his outlook, and his fondness for fish with one of his Hindu colleagues than he would with a Karachi Shia or Pashtun Sufi from the North-West Frontier." Historian Yasmin Khan agrees: "There was no such thing as one Muslim, Hindu or Sikh community in South Asia," she writes, noting that "linguistic and cultural differences zigzagged across the country."

This changed once India came under the control of the East India Company and, later, the British government. "Generations of European administrators, travelers, and scholars foregrounded the 'spiritual' in all their interpretations of India and, in their eyes, Hindus, Muslims and Sikhs were inescapably separate and mutually incompatible," explains Y. Khan.

This had several effects. When "the British started to define 'communities' based on religious identity and attach political representation to them," writes historian Alex von Tunzelmann, "many Indians … began to ask themselves in which of the boxes they belonged." Another effect of viewing Hindus, Muslims, and Sikhs as separate communities was that it often prompted British officials to implement, as Y. Khan writes, "well-intentioned policies intended to show British fair play and even-handedness," many of which ended up "encouraging co-religionists to bond more tightly together."

Then there were those policies that were not so well-intentioned. British officials in India understood that the most efficient way to govern a population as diverse and unruly as India's was to divide it—in particular, to separate the Hindus from the Muslims. "The creation and perpetuation of Hindu-Muslim antagonism was the most significant accomplishment of British imperial policy: the colonial project of 'divide et impera' (divide and rule) fomented religious antagonisms to facilitate continued imperial rule," writes journalist Shashi Tharoor.

The partition of Bengal in 1905 is a key example of this divisive approach. Indeed, it appears that its express purpose was to pit Hindu and Muslim communities against each other. As one British official, H. H. Risley, observed, "Bengal united is a power. Bengal divided will pull in several different ways … One of our main objects is to split up and thereby weaken a solid body of opponents to our rule." Lord Curzon concurred, noting in a letter to India's secretary of state that the British Raj must "divide the Bengali-speaking population." Curzon knew such a maneuver would be "intensely and hotly resented by them," adding that "the outcry will be loud and very fierce." But, he concluded, "as a native gentleman said to me—'my countrymen always howl until a thing is settled; then they accept it.'"

The outcry was indeed loud and fierce—among Hindus, at least. Indeed, Hindus on both sides of the new provincial border vehemently protested the maneuver: those on the Muslim-majority side, in East Bengal and Assam, resented their diminished clout, while those in West Bengal resented their loss of control over the natural resources they needed to run their mills and factories. However, Muslims were more accepting of the partition. They quickly grasped the advantage of having a Muslim majority in East Bengal and Assam. As for the Muslims in West Bengal, they had always been the minority there. For them, nothing had changed.

Public opposition to this partition—and a subsequent boycott of foreign goods by Hindus across India—prompted British officials to stitch the two provinces back together in 1911. Still, the maneuver had struck a significant blow to Hindu-Muslim relations in the region.

The Formation of the Muslim League

In 1906, growing unrest and division among Hindus and Muslims prompted members of the Muslim elite to meet with the Earl of Minto, who had replaced Lord Curzon as viceroy. They asked that the British Raj institute separate electorates for different religious groups and allot a set number of seats in government to Muslim candidates. In this way, they could ensure representation for the Muslim minority in the ever-evolving Indian government.

Their goal became a reality with the passage of the Indian Councils Act 1909, also called the Morley-Minto Reforms. While the law proved advantageous for the Muslim population, it had an important negative side effect, "embed[ding] deeply in Indian life the idea that its society consisted of groups set apart from each other." This shift would have significant repercussions in the years to come.

Many of the same Muslim elites who pushed for separate electorates also joined together to form a new political party, called the All India Muslim League (later known as simply the Muslim League). Unlike the Indian National Congress—a party that claimed to stand for all Indians regardless of religion or ethnicity—the Muslim League focused only on the needs of the country's Muslim population. Interestingly, many members of the Muslim League were also members of the Congress—at least at first—indicating a degree of unity among the two parties.

The Muslim League was not the only group devoted to serving the interests of India's Muslim population. However, over time, it grew to eclipse all the others. By the 1940s, the Muslim League would become an unstoppable force in Indian politics and the driving force behind partition and the formation of Pakistan.

World War I and the Push for Dominion Status

July 1914 brought the advent of World War I. During the war, 1.4 million members of the British Indian Army fought bravely alongside other Allied forces. Most Indian

The Muslim League met for the first time in 1906. Like the Indian National Congress, the Muslim League would become an important political body.

The Long Road to Indian Independence

Indian soldiers are pictured in the trenches during World War I.

28   The Partition of India

soldiers were stationed in Africa and the Middle East, but some shipped out as far away as Europe. Roughly seventy-four thousand died.

The Indian people did more than contribute military might to the Allied effort. They also supplied food, ammunition, and—thanks to high taxes imposed by the British—money. Indians believed that, in return, the British would endow India with dominion status, as it had with such countries as Canada, Australia, New Zealand, and South Africa. Dominions were countries that had once been part of the British Empire. They had since been granted sovereignty but remained part of a loose federation of nations with special ties to Britain. This federation was called the Commonwealth.

Indians had good reason to believe they would soon be granted such a status. In December 1916, the Muslim League and the Congress issued a joint resolution that "His Majesty the King Emperor [King George V] should be pleased to issue a proclamation announcing that it is the aim and intention of British Policy to confer self-government on India at an early date" and "that in the reconstruction of the Empire, India should be lifted from the position of a dependency to that of an equal partner in the Empire with self-governing Dominions."

That same year, leaders of both parties also signed an important document called the Lucknow Pact. This pact called for a "scheme of reforms" that, in the interim, would transfer certain governing powers to Indian officials. Proposed reforms included an increase in the number of Indian representatives on provincial legislative councils and on the Imperial Legislative Council and an expansion of these representatives' role. The pact also suggested that "adequate provision should be made for the representation of important minorities by election, and that Mahomedans [Muslims] should be represented through special electorates on the Provincial Legislative Council."

The practice of dividing the electorate by religion to ensure the election of Muslim representatives echoed the Morley-Minto Reforms of 1909. However, the Lucknow Pact represented a significant step toward unity between the Congress and the Muslim League on the matter.

It also united both parties in the larger fight for Indian autonomy. As Congress leader Gangadhar Tilak explained, "When we have to fight against a third party—it is a very important thing that we stand on this platform united, united in race, united in religion, as regards to all different shades of political creed."

The Montagu-Chelmsford Reforms

In the end, Indians who longed for self-rule in the aftermath of World War I were sorely disappointed. It's true that in 1919, India passed legislation that was, according to Secretary of State Edwin Montagu, geared toward increasing Indian presence "in every branch of the administration, and the gradual development of self-governing institutions, with a view to the progressive realisation of responsible government in India as an integral part of the British Empire." This legislation—called the Government of India Act 1919, or the Montagu-Chelmsford Reforms—gave Indians their best chance yet to acquire legislative power, especially at the provincial level.

However, the reforms were also hampered by the (still) limited number of eligible voters. Worse, it eliminated all hope for self-rule. Tilak described the legislation as "unsatisfactory and disappointing—a sunless dawn." Activist Annie Beasant deemed it "unworthy of England to offer and India to accept."

As if all that weren't bad enough, the legislation was also undercut by an extension of the Defense of India Act 1915. This law—passed in the throes of the First World War—allowed government officials to suppress sedition using a variety of means, such as silencing or censoring the press, arresting individuals suspected of treason without a warrant, and detaining anti-England activists without trial. The extension, called the Rowlatt Act, passed despite public outcry and a lack of support from Montagu, who wrote to the viceroy, "I do most awfully want to help you stamp out rebellion and revolution, but I loathe the suggestion at first sight of preserving the Defense of India Act in peacetime … Why cannot these things be done by normal, or even exceptional processes of law?"

Social Unrest and the Ascent of Mahatma Gandhi

The passage of the Rowlatt Act spurred civil unrest throughout India. Public protests proliferated nationwide. The British response to these protests was both swift and merciless, as in April 1919, when some fifty British soldiers opened fire on thousands of peaceful protesters—men, women, and children—in a public garden in the city of Amritsar. The British government in India reported some 379 civilian deaths; the Congress calculated a casualty rate of three times that many. Incredibly, although the British government relieved the commander of the soldiers, Brigadier General Reginald E. H. Dyer, from duty

Right: Mohandas K. Gandhi (*seated at center*) became a key leader in the movement for Indian independence.

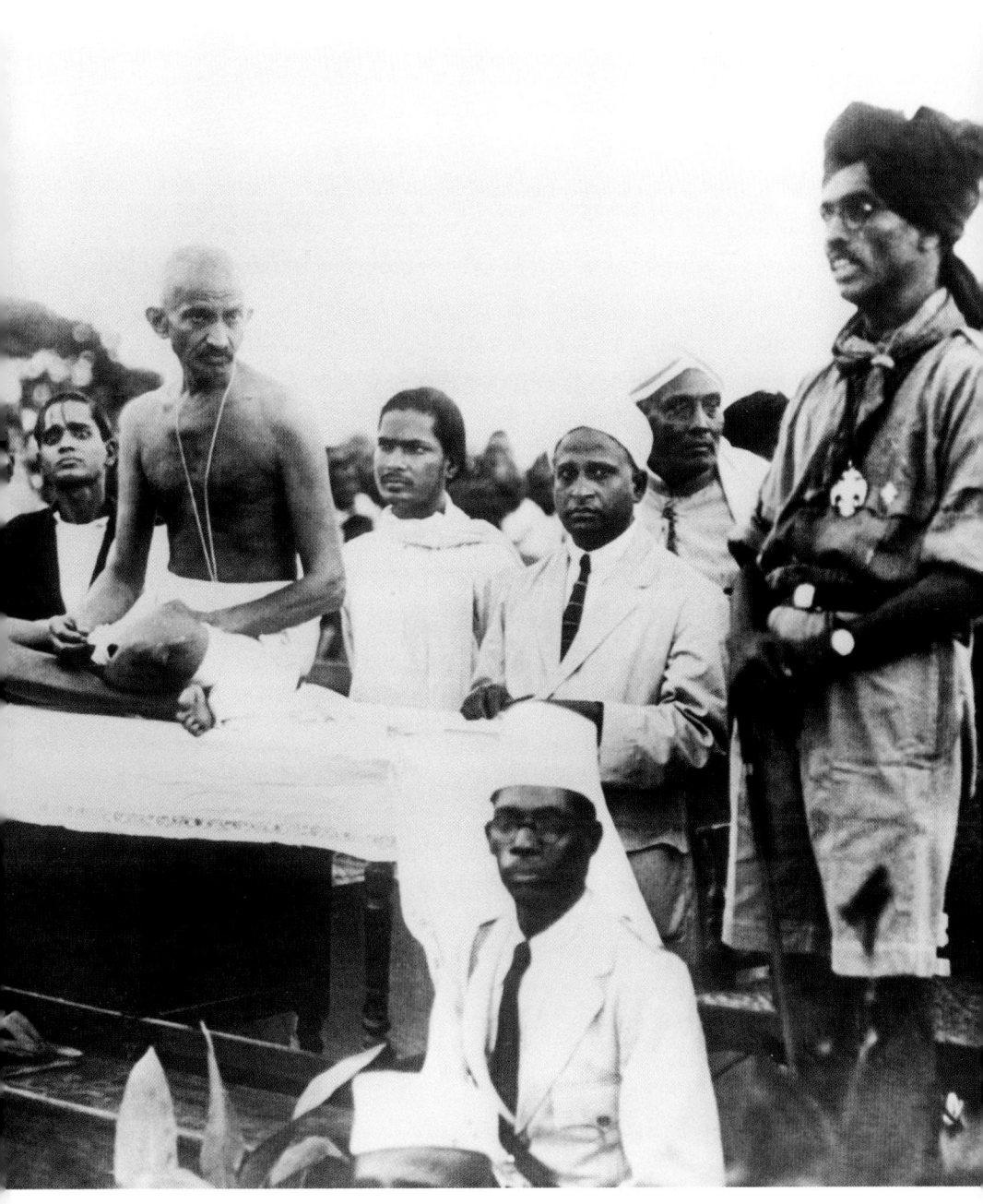

following the so-called Amritsar Massacre (also known as the Jallianwala Bagh Massacre), members of the British public hailed him as a hero.

For many Indians, the Amritsar Massacre represented a breaking point. They would no longer be mollified by empty promises of self-rule. The massacre also solidified the position of an emerging Indian leader: Mohandas K. Gandhi. Born in western India into a Hindu merchant family, Gandhi studied law in London before emigrating to another outpost of the British Empire, South Africa. There, Gandhi organized nonviolent protests to gain civil rights for his fellow Indians abroad.

In 1915, Gandhi returned to India intent on spreading his philosophy of nonviolent resistance. Gandhi called this practice *satyagraha*, or "striving for truth," and described it as the "last resort of those strong enough in their commitment to truth to undergo suffering in its cause."

Gandhi's goal was not to achieve self-rule, or *swaraj*, for India—at least, not at first. Rather, Gandhi's cause was improving the lives of Indians of all castes and faiths. To that end, he launched several peaceful protests. One occurred in Bihar on behalf of tenant farmers whose landlords forced them to plant indigo crops, then purchased the indigo under market value. Another took place in Kaira on behalf of land-owning farmers subject to heavy taxes. A third protest was on behalf of textile workers in Ahmedabad who sought higher wages.

Following the Amritsar Massacre, however, Gandhi's views on Indian self-rule changed. He believed that "a society must be built in which every village has to be self-sustained and capable of managing its own affairs ... This does not exclude dependence on and willing help from neighbors or from the world. [But] it will be a free and voluntary play of mutual forces." To achieve swaraj, Gandhi launched a program called the noncooperation movement in 1920. Followers of this nonviolent movement boycotted British goods, opting instead for local handicrafts.

The noncooperation movement lasted for just two years, ending when British authorities arrested Gandhi and sentenced him to six years in prison. (He served only two.) This did not end Indians' desire for independence, however—in fact, their desires intensified.

As for Gandhi, he would remain an important— even revered—figure in India, earning the title mahatma, from the Sanskrit word *mahatman*, or "great-souled." On January 30, 1948, Gandhi was shot and killed by a Hindu nationalist named Nathuram Godse, who believed Gandhi should not have accommodated Muslim demands and blamed him for the ensuing suffering during partition. Indians and Pakistanis alike were saddened by this turn of events. More than two million people participated in a funeral procession in New Delhi, and many shopkeepers in Pakistan closed their shops to show their respect.

CHAPTER THREE

Partition

During the 1920s, relations between the Muslim League and the Indian National Congress cooled. Both groups continued to work toward self-governance in a free and united India, but by 1930, some members of the Muslim League had shifted from this objective. They no longer sought a single Indian state, in which communities of Hindus, Muslims, Sikhs, and others were tightly intertwined. Rather, they called for a separate Muslim homeland. This change set the subcontinent on the long road to partition and an independent Pakistan.

The Pakistan Movement, and a Shift Toward Independence

The Muslim League's policy shift came in response to growing concerns about the unfair treatment

Sir Muhammad Iqbal became president of the Muslim League in 1930 and was among the first to push for a Muslim homeland.

of Muslims by Hindu-majority leadership, which governed much of India despite efforts to increase Muslim representation. As historian Ian Talbot notes, "The provincial Congress governments made no effort to understand and respect their Muslim populations' cultural and religious sensibilities."

The situation was exacerbated by scarce resources. "If people could not get hold of resources, it was all too easy to attribute blame to the party in power," historian Yasmin Khan observes. Many people in Congress-governed provinces came to believe that only Congress followers would have access to food and essential supplies. In League-run provinces, the reverse was also true. Because of these divisions, Sir Muhammad Iqbal, who became president of the Muslim League in 1930, came to believe that establishing a Muslim homeland would be "the only course by which we can secure a peaceful India and save Muslims from the domination of Non-Muslims."

At first, Muslim nationalists like Iqbal envisioned a province, as Iqbal described it, a "Muslim India within India." This would require the joining of several regions in northwest India into a single Muslim state. To Iqbal, whether that state existed "within the British Empire or without the British Empire" was immaterial, so long as it enjoyed self-rule. Soon, however, this vision gave way to a call for a separate and independent Muslim nation, named Pakistan. *Pakistan* was short for *P*unjab, *A*fghania, *K*ashmir, *S*indh, and Baluchis*tan*— the regions of India that Muslim nationalists sought to claim as their own. It means "land of the pure" in Persian and Urdu, languages commonly used among Muslims.

This "two-nation theory," as it was called, provided the underpinnings for the Pakistan movement and, ultimately, partition. It stemmed from the notion that religion, rather than language, ethnicity, or even geography, dictated national identity—particularly for Muslims. In a speech before the Muslim League, Iqbal noted that in Islam, religious ideals were inextricably tied to social order, "therefore, the construction of a policy on national lines, if it means a displacement of the Islamic principle of solidarity, is simply unthinkable to a Muslim."

The Congress vehemently opposed the Pakistan movement. To them, says Y. Khan, "Pakistan was perceived as a total and sweeping threat which risked shattering the whole of Mother India." It was, she continues, "akin to dismantling the promise of a free India altogether" and "risked opening the floodgates to further national disintegration and secessionist movements." Initially, even some Muslims viewed the notion of a Muslim homeland with skepticism, calling it "chimerical and impracticable"—an impossible

THE CENSUS OF 1901

In 1901 the British Raj conducted a census in India. It showed the total population was 294 million people. Of these, roughly 207 million were Hindu, 63 million were Muslim, 9 million were Buddhist, 3 million were Christian, 2 million were Sikh, and 1 million were Jain.

MUHAMMAD ALI JINNAH

Mohammad Ali Jinnah served as the on-again, off-again president of the Muslim League starting in 1916 and ending in 1947.

Jinnah was born in 1876 to a merchant family in Karachi. In 1892, after an arranged marriage, Jinnah moved to England to study law, where he developed an interest in politics. His wife died while he was abroad. After Jinnah returned to India in 1896 to start a law practice in Bombay, he followed Indian politics closely. In 1904, he joined the Indian National Congress.

At first, Jinnah opposed the formation of the Muslim League. He also opposed the institution of separate electorates based on religion—even though these separate electorates helped him win his seat on the Imperial Legislative Council in 1909. Eventually, Jinnah's stance on the Muslim League softened. He joined the party in 1913, although he considered it to be secondary in importance to the Congress, of which he remained a member.

In 1918, Jinnah married again. The couple separated in 1929, and his wife died soon after, leaving their daughter in the care of Jinnah and his sister.

By 1920, Jinnah's political priorities had flipped. A rift with party leaders prompted him to abandon the Congress and focus full-time on the Muslim League. Jinnah also abandoned the movement for a united India to push for a Muslim homeland, despite the fact that Jinnah himself was, in the words of journalist William Dalrymple, "a staunch secularist [who] drank whiskey, rarely went to a mosque, and was clean-shaven and stylish, favoring beautifully cut Savile Row suits and silk ties."

Jinnah's vision for Pakistan became a reality with partition in 1947. Afterward, Jinnah became the first governor-general of Pakistan. He held this title for only one year, however. In September 1948, suffering from tuberculosis, pneumonia, and advanced lung cancer (he was known to smoke more than fifty cigarettes a day), Jinnah died at the age of seventy-one.

Mohammad Ali Jinnah (*left*) is pictured with Mohandas K. Gandhi. Jinnah is seen as the founder of Pakistan.

Jinnah's death had profound consequences, "depriv[ing] Pakistan of a leader who could have enhanced stability and democratic governance," historian Yasmeen Niaz Mohiuddin explains. "The rocky road to democracy in Pakistan and the relatively smooth one in India can in some measure be ascribed to Pakistan's tragedy of losing an incorruptible and highly revered leader so soon after independence."

Today, writes Yasmin Khan, Jinnah is "widely reviled [by Indians] as the progenitor of Pakistan and the architect of a mistaken partition of the subcontinent." Pakistanis, however, "cherish his memory as their greatest leader and the founder of their Muslim state." Perhaps biographer Stanley Wolpert summarizes Jinnah's impact best: "Few individuals significantly alter the course of history. Fewer still modify the map of the world. Hardly anyone can be credited with creating a nation-state. Mohammad Ali Jinnah did all three."

dream. Eventually, however, the idea caught on among many Muslims in India. Indeed, observes Y. Khan, the notion of Pakistan grew from a simple territorial claim to signify "a utopian future for many Muslims."

The Government of India Act 1935

One provision of the Government of India Act 1919 called for the British government to send a special commission to India ten years after the act's passage to assess its impact. To that end, in 1928, a group of seven members of British Parliament, called the Simon Commission (after its chairman, Sir John Allsebrook Simon), gathered in India to study the state of affairs and to institute reforms. The failure to include even a single Indian member in the Simon Commission incensed the Indian populace, spurring strikes and even violent protests, and prompting a boycott by both the Congress and the Muslim League.

The impact of the commission was not immediately felt. However, its ultimate outcome was the passage of the Government of India Act 1935 by the British Parliament. This act allowed for direct elections and expanded voting rights to include women and members of lower castes, increasing the number of eligible voters to thirty-five million (still a relatively small number, given that the population of India was roughly ten times this size). The act also instituted a bicameral parliament consisting of the Council of State and the Central Assembly; established a federal court; and introduced the Reserve Bank of India to control monetary policy. Finally, it allowed Indians to elect as many of their countrymen to the provincial governments as they wished—although they were permitted to vote only for those candidates in their social or religious category (for example, landholder, lower caste, Muslim, and so on). This act would later serve as the foundation of the Indian constitution.

The first election after these rules took effect occurred in 1937. The Congress—whose manifesto still deemphasized religion in favor of economic and social issues—handily won eight of the eleven provinces in India. The Muslim League, however, fared poorly—even losing seats reserved for Muslims to Muslim members of the Congress.

The Lahore Resolution

By March 1940, Mohammad Ali Jinnah, an Indian Muslim politician and Muslim League leader, had wholly committed to the two-nation theory and the Pakistan movement. That month, he delivered an important address before the Muslim League in the city of Lahore, stating:

> Islam and Hinduism … are not religions in the strict sense of the word, but are, in fact, different and distinct social orders; and it is a dream that the Hindus and Muslims can ever evolve a common nationality; and this misconception of one Indian nation has gone far beyond the limits and is the cause of more of our

troubles and will lead India to destruction if we fail to revise our notions in time.

Jinnah continued:

The Hindus and Muslims belong to two different religious philosophies, social customs, and literature[s]. They neither intermarry nor interdine together, and indeed they belong to two different civilisations which are based mainly on conflicting ideas and conceptions … To yoke together two such nations under a single state, one as a numerical minority and the other as a majority, must lead to growing discontent and final destruction of any fabric that may be so built for the government of such a state.

At this same gathering, the Muslim League adopted a resolution, called the Lahore Resolution or the Pakistan Resolution. This resolution demanded that "the areas in which the Muslims are numerically a majority as in the North-Western and Eastern zones of India should be grouped to constitute 'Independent States' in which the constituent units shall be autonomous and sovereign." In other words, it called for an independent and autonomous Pakistan.

Leaders of the Congress scoffed at the resolution. The president of the Congress, Jawaharlal Nehru, called the demands "Jinnah's fantastic proposals" ("fantastic," in this case, meaning "bizarre" or "fanciful" rather than "wonderful" or "amazing"). Another party leader, Chakravarti Rajagopalachari, suggested Jinnah's

It wasn't just Indian men who served during World War II. Indian women did, too.

push for Pakistan was "a sign of a diseased mentality." Gandhi was more sanguine. He conceded that Muslims, like all Indians, had a right to self-governance—although he did describe the resolution as "baffling."

World War II and the Ascension of the Muslim League

At the onset of World War II, Congress leaders were shocked and outraged when, without consulting them,

Indian soldiers are pictured in Burma during World War II.

the British declared war on India's behalf and sent more than two million Indian troops into battle. Some members of the Congress even resigned their posts in protest.

During the war, Indian troops, stationed primarily in North Africa and the Middle East, served a critical role in numerous Allied campaigns. However, India contributed more than just soldiers to the war effort. As it had in World War I, India also produced uniforms and munitions for British forces, including rifles, machine guns, field artillery, and ammunition, as well as warships and aircraft.

In March 1942, grasping the importance of these contributions and sensing a deepening rift between the Congress and the British government, British leaders sent a delegation to India to ensure the continued cooperation of Indian leaders in the war effort. In return for their aid, the delegation, led by Sir Richard Stafford Cripps, was empowered to grant India limited dominion status after the war. However, this so-called Cripps Mission failed to address a timetable for the handover, nor did it clearly enumerate which powers the British would relinquish. For these and other reasons, the Congress rejected the delegation's offer, memorably described by Gandhi as a "postdated check on a failing bank."

Leaders of the Muslim League reacted differently. The Muslim League did not overtly support the war effort; however, unlike the Congress, it did not actively attempt to obstruct it, either. One unforeseen outcome of this stance was that British officials increasingly viewed Jinnah as being on equal footing with such Congress leaders as Gandhi. This left Jinnah, in his own words, "wonderstruck." The British also came to look upon the Muslim League as the main representative of Muslims in India, despite the existence of many other Muslim political groups. Clearly, as Jinnah later admitted, "The war which nobody welcomed proved to be a blessing in disguise."

Gandhi launched the Quit India movement at this demonstration in Bombay (now Mumbai).

Quit India

Following the failed Cripps Mission, Gandhi launched a new movement for Indian independence called Quit India. This campaign demanded drastic changes to the Indian constitution and called for an immediate end to the British Raj. "Ours is not a drive for power, but purely a nonviolent fight for India's independence," Gandhi explained during a speech before members of the Congress in August 1942. "In the democracy which I have envisaged, a democracy established by nonviolence, there will be equal freedom for all. Everybody will be his own master ... Once you realize this you will forget the differences between Hindus and Muslims, and think of yourselves as Indians only, engaged in the common struggle for independence."

The British still had their hands full on the European continent, mired as they were in World War II. Still, they quickly crushed Quit India. Within hours of Gandhi's speech before the Congress, British officials had imprisoned tens of thousands of Congress officials at the local, provincial, and national level—including Gandhi himself. Most of these officials would remain imprisoned for the duration of the war. The British banned the Congress and violently extinguished all demonstrations on behalf of the Quit India movement, arresting more than one hundred thousand agitators and even subjecting some to public flogging.

Crushing the Quit India movement triggered some unintended consequences—among these, in the words of Y. Khan, "a definite streak of anti-Europeanism" among the Indian populace, particularly against British government officials. As one such official wrote to the viceroy in 1945, "I am bound to say that I cannot recollect any period in which there have been such venomous and unbridled attacks against government and government officers."

Another unintended consequence of the Quit India movement's demise was a significant improvement in the fortunes of the Muslim League. With tens of thousands of Congress officials jailed and the party banned, there was no one to challenge leaders of the Muslim League as they stoked fears of Hindu domination over minority Muslim populations and argued for the creation of Pakistan.

A Shift in Policy

In the years before and during World War II, Britain had demonstrated reluctance to fully surrender its claim on India, even as it included more and more Indians in the political and governing processes. By the end of the war, however, this reluctance was gone. Indeed, British leaders wanted to rid the empire of the Raj—and fast. This was due in large part to "Britain's precarious economic position in the aftermath of the war," scholar Lucy Chester explains. "After nearly two centuries as an economic asset, British India had become a liability at a time when Britain could least afford it." In other words, its coffers drained by the war effort, Britain had little choice but to surrender the "jewel in its crown," India.

In 1945, King George VI of England announced the impending split during an address before the British Parliament. "In accordance with the promises already made to my Indian peoples," the king said,

King George VI (*left*) is pictured alongside British prime minister Clement Attlee.

"my government will do their utmost to promote, in conjunction with the leaders of Indian opinion, the early realization of full self-government in India." Indeed, according to Y. Khan, "it was only a fortnight after Victory Week in Delhi ... that the members of the British delegation, sent to negotiate a constitutional settlement for India, and to plan its disengagement from empire, arrived at the capital."

The British were clearly ready to cut their losses. Their only sticking point was how to avoid blame for the growing conflict between Hindus and Muslims. "For those engineering the transfer of power," notes Y. Khan, "in keeping with the British ideal of democratic decolonization, the answer was an Indian general election."

The Election of 1946

When World War II ended in 1945, British officials released the tens of thousands of Congress leaders who had been imprisoned for instigating the Quit India movement. "On their release," says Y. Khan, "the leadership was 'thrown into a new world.'" She continues, "Indians ecstatically greeted their pantheon of heroes but Nehru and the others had fallen out of step with the popular politics of the moment."

The "popular politics" revolved around one key issue: the long-awaited transfer of power from British to Indian officials, mandated by King George VI and set into motion by Britain's new prime minister, Clement

Attlee. To facilitate this transfer, the British government had called for a new election, the purpose of which was twofold, according to Y. Khan. First, it was "to form provincial governments in the Indian provinces, and so draw Indian politicians into the business of running the everyday functions of government from which Congress had been excluded during the Second World War." Second, it was "to create a body that would start designing the future constitutional form of a free India." Between December 1945 and March 1946, tens of millions of Indian citizens cast their votes.

In the run-up to the election, leaders of the Muslim League ran a single-issue campaign—and that single issue was Pakistan. Indeed, the election became, in effect, a referendum on Pakistani nationhood. As Jinnah told one group, "Pakistan is a matter of life or death for us." He warned another that voting against the Muslim League would result in Hindu Raj—that is, Hindu rule in India.

The League's efforts paid off. The party won 75 percent of the Muslim vote in the provincial elections—up from just over 4 percent in 1937—and claimed majorities in Bengal, Punjab, and Sindh. What's more, it won all the Muslim seats in the Central Assembly (although this was not enough to wrest control of this body from the Congress). This, in the words of Stanley Wolpert, "appeared to prove the universal appeal of Pakistan among Muslims of the subcontinent." It should be noted, however, that only a limited number of Indians—including Muslims—were permitted to vote, meaning we can't really know just how universally appealing Pakistan truly was.

The Cabinet Mission

Those Muslims in India who were eligible to vote might have opted overwhelmingly for partition and Pakistan, but the British, like the Congress, preferred a united India. In an attempt to broker a compromise, the British government dispatched another delegation to India in March 1946 in a "last push for peace."

In May, the delegation, called the Cabinet Mission, set forth a proposal for a united India: the ABC Plan. It suggested a loose federation of provinces, grouped together by religion. These provinces—which, according to the plan, would be free to secede from the union if they chose—would be largely autonomous, although a central government would handle such matters as defense. The plan also mandated the installation of an interim government composed of members of both the Congress and the Muslim League. Y. Khan notes that it was, "in some ways, a genuine compromise that allowed for a sharing of land and a division of people and materials." It also "acknowledged the right to self-determination of a large group of Muslims who … had expressed their strong desire to extricate themselves from the Congress's control."

Jinnah was not averse to the ABC Plan. Nor were a significant number of Muslims in India. For many, says Y. Khan, "this version of 'Pakistan' was good enough."

The Congress, however, balked at the notion of a largely decentralized government. Some members of the Congress were angry that the proposal made any concessions to the Muslim League at all. What's more, neither party could agree on the number of representatives they would install in the interim government. The members of the Cabinet Mission insisted that the Congress and the Muslim League either accept or reject the ABC Plan in its entirety—no modifications allowed. So the plan, in the end, was rejected.

Ultimately, says Y. Khan, the delegation's inability to broker a compromise was the result of "a failure of trust." Both the Congress and the Muslim League were "unwilling to take the leap into an unknown future without cast-iron guarantees that the plan would be interpreted in precisely the same way by all parties once the British had departed." That, plus the "reasonable doubts—based on past disappointments—about the British intention finally to relinquish its Indian empire after two centuries" doomed the effort.

Things Fall Apart

After the failure of the Cabinet Mission, Jinnah proclaimed August 16, 1946, to be a holiday, called Direct Action Day. The stated purpose of this holiday was to peacefully demonstrate Muslim support for Pakistan. Sadly, Direct Action Day devolved into something else entirely.

The trouble began in Calcutta. There, thousands of Muslims gathered to hear a speech by the chief

In August 1946, riots consumed Calcutta for three days, resulting in the deaths of some four thousand Hindus and Muslims.

minister of the Muslim League in Bengal, Husseyn Suhrawardy. According to Y. Khan, Suhrawardy's speech "did not explicitly incite violence." However, the speech "certainly gave the crowds the impression that [Muslims] could act with impunity, that neither the police nor the military would be called out and that the ministry would turn a blind eye to any action they unleashed in the city." Suhrawardy also conveyed this message to a local newspaper, adding that "bloodshed and disorder are not necessarily evil in themselves, if resorted to for a noble cause."

Over the next three days, violence between Muslims and Hindus consumed Calcutta. In the final tally, some four thousand residents of Calcutta lay dead, with more than ten thousand injured. No one was spared on either side—not women, not children, not the elderly. "Ordinary people going about their daily business were targeted," says Y. Khan, "from tea-shop owners and rickshaw drivers to stallholders who had been dragged out, beaten and burned or had their property looted." Afterward, she observes, "the scene was one of carnage … A British official groped for an analogy, describing the landscape as a cross between the worst of London air raids and the Great Plague." American photojournalist Margaret Bourke-White agreed, writing that the streets of Calcutta "looked like Buchenwald," the German concentration camp.

The Calcutta Killings, as the riot came to be known, sparked yet more violence between Muslims and Hindus elsewhere in India, including in East Bengal, Bihar, and the United Provinces. With each new outbreak, political leaders in the Congress and Muslim League found themselves less and less able to contain it. For their part, British officials denied responsibility for this widespread violence.

These riots—in which Muslims and Hindus both instigated and suffered from violence in equal measure—proved to be a turning point, both politically and psychologically. In the words of Y. Khan, they "reinforced, in a graphic way, the idea that Hindus and

Muslims were incompatible, and planted this seed in the minds of British and Indian policymakers."

The Push for Partition

Muslims and Hindus found themselves trapped in an ongoing cycle of violence. Gandhi himself warned, "We are not yet in the midst of a civil war. But we are nearing it." Canadian writer and comparative religion scholar Wilfred Cantwell Smith agreed: "Of late the situation in India has deteriorated menacingly … Instead of an India with freedom for all, united in friendly communal partnership, there have been signs pointing to, at best, a stagnant India of intense mutual bickering, on problems of constitutions and of problems of daily bread, within an atmosphere of moral degradation and of riots; and at worst, an India of civil war."

Before long, these constant clashes between Muslims and Hindus forced leaders of the Congress to reconsider their stance on partition. "The truth," Nehru later admitted, "is that we were tired men and we were getting on in years … The plan for partition offered a way out and we took it." Other Indians of many political persuasions soon followed suit.

Partition not only offered Hindu leaders a way to avoid civil war. It also allowed them the freedom to reshape India as they saw fit—without taking Muslim priorities into account. As one Congress leader noted, "for the first time since [the twelfth century], we had received the opportunity to develop the country according to what could broadly be called Hindu ideals."

British leaders were likewise convinced. Once the Congress saw partition "as a pathway out of the interminable political morass," says Y. Khan, "it was only a matter of time before the creation of two separate states took on momentum in the thinking of the viceroy and his advisors."

Attlee and Mountbatten

On February 20, 1947, British prime minister Clement Attlee announced that Great Britain would indeed grant India's independence, with the transfer of power to occur no later than June 1948—just sixteen months away. Some British officials viewed this plan with skepticism and alarm. Attlee's predecessor, Winston Churchill, described the timetable as a "hurried scuttle" and a "shameful flight"—the consequences of which, notes author Mahboobul Rahman Khan, "would fall wholly upon the peoples of India." Attlee made no mention of partition in his announcement, however. "London's aim was to cut British losses, by leaving a united India if possible, a divided India if not," Y. Khan explains. Attlee also announced the appointment of a new viceroy to plan the transition: a career naval officer named Lord Louis Mountbatten.

Over a period of six days in April 1947, Mountbatten met with Jinnah to hammer out the

Jawaharlal Nehru (*left*), Lord Mountbatten (*second from right*), and Muhammad Ali Jinnah (*right*) are pictured during negotiations regarding the partition of India.

issue of partition. He quickly ascertained that, as his advisors had warned him, Jinnah would be his "toughest customer." No matter what approach Mountbatten took to persuade Jinnah to accept a united India, Jinnah did not budge. Finally, even though Mountbatten considered the very idea of Pakistan to be "sheer madness," he gave up. "It had become clear," he told Attlee in May, "that the Muslim League would resort to arms if Pakistan in some form were not conceded."

On June 3, 1947, Mountbatten issued his plan for the transfer of power. This plan, named the

Mountbatten Plan, called for the creation of two independent states: India and Pakistan. The plan also called for the creation of a commission to determine the boundaries between these states. But that wasn't all. As noted, Attlee had given a June 1948 deadline for the transfer of power. Mountbatten moved that deadline up by almost a year. Now, the transfer would occur on August 15, 1947—just seventy-three days away.

Gandhi vehemently opposed the Mountbatten Plan. He called partition the "vivisection of the Mother"— but he was overruled.

The Congress, led by Nehru, signed off on the plan. So, too, did the Muslim League, led by Jinnah. On July 18, it was rubber-stamped by the British government with the passage of the Indian Independence Act 1947.

And so it was done.

TWO REGIONS, ONE PAKISTAN

When Pakistan at last came into being, it consisted of two large swathes of land. One was West Pakistan, northwest of India. The other was East Pakistan, 1,000 miles (1,608 km) to the east. A diplomat named K. M. Panikkar likened the resulting map to an elephant and its ears: "Hindustan [India] is the elephant … and Pakistan the two ears." But, he added, "the elephant can live without the ears."

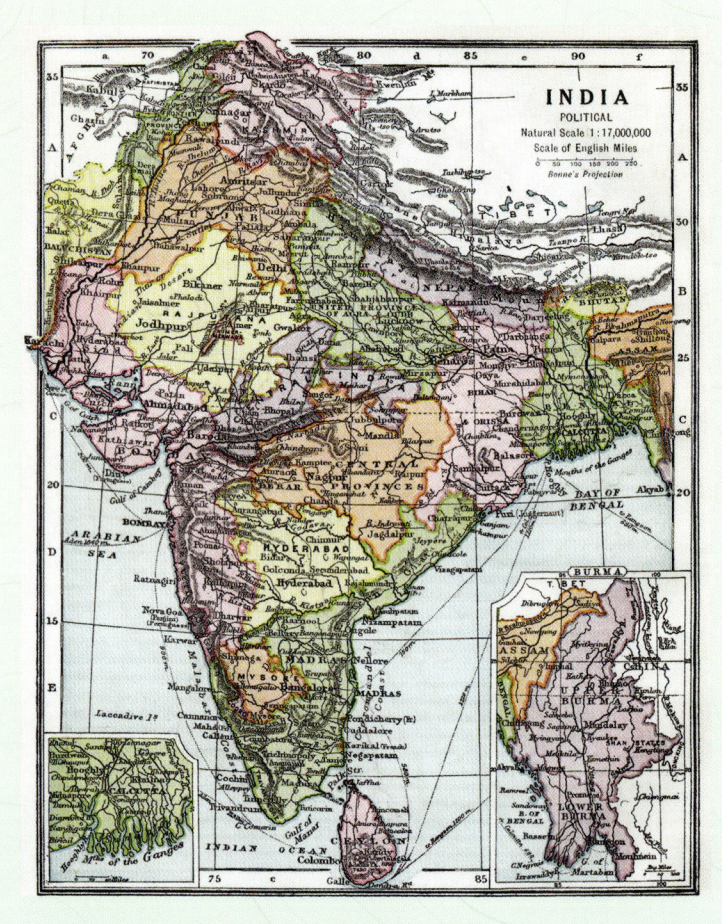

The Indian subcontinent is shown before partition.

Together, West Pakistan and East Pakistan comprised 565,493 square miles (904,790 sq km). This was roughly one-third of the size of post-partition India, which covered 1,856,250 square miles (2,970,000 sq km), which was appropriate, given the difference in the two countries' populations. In the years following partition, Pakistan was home to an estimated 75 million people, whereas 361 million people—more than five times that number—lived in India.

In 1971, Pakistan's land and population would shrink as East Pakistan gained independence and became known as Bangladesh.

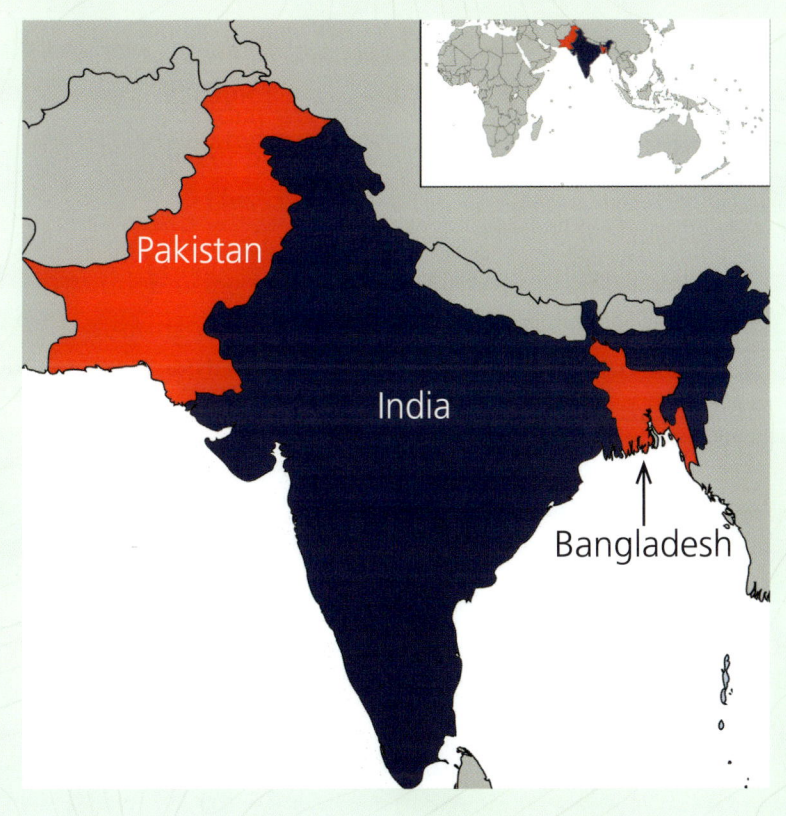

The Indian subcontinent is shown as it is today.

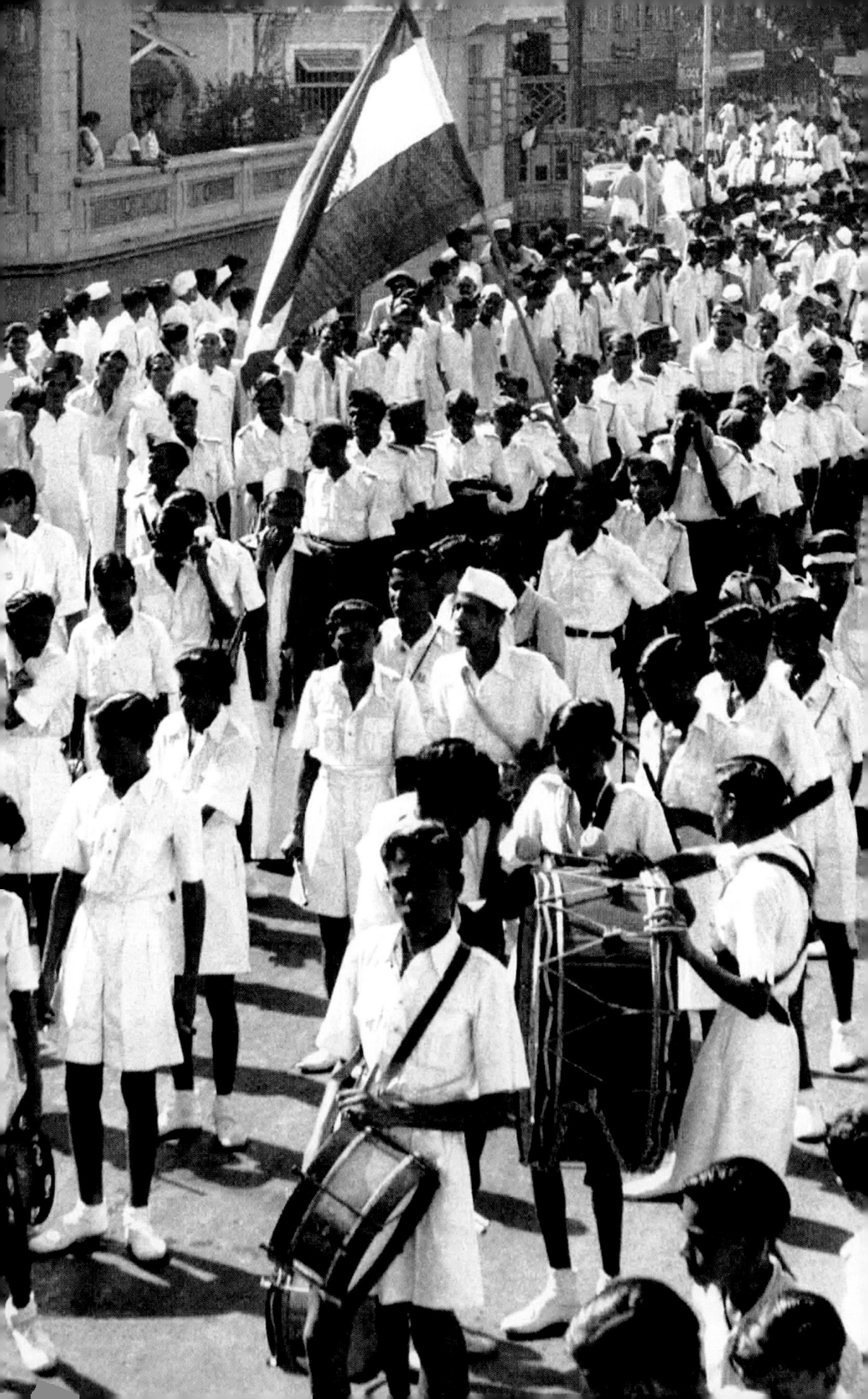

CHAPTER FOUR
The Radcliffe Line

The Mountbatten Plan allowed just seventy-three days to disentangle India from Britain; to split land, assets, and armies between India and Pakistan; and to undo nearly two hundred years of British rule. It was, says historian Stanley Wolpert, "cut and run, full speed ahead." The transition would be a difficult one for all parties involved, particularly when it came to drawing the new borders.

"Cut and Run"

As author Mahboobul Rahman Khan observes in his paper, "Mountbatten and the 'Hurried Scuttle,'" "Mountbatten could not possibly [have been] unaware of the magnitude of the tasks involved in partitioning India and setting up two independent states, the

Left: Bombay (now Mumbai) celebrates Independence Day on August 15, 1947.

The front page of the *Hindustan Times* announces Independence Day.

inadequacy of the time available and the necessity of accomplishing them in an orderly way, a little, if not well ahead of the actual transfer of power." It's therefore reasonable to wonder why, given these realities,

Mountbatten chose to compress the timetable so dramatically—or indeed at all.

Some historians suggest that the escalating violence between Hindus and Muslims—and the inability of the British army, weakened by war, to contain it—led to the decision. Indeed, Mountbatten himself said, "The only conclusion that I have been able to come to is that unless I act quickly I may well find the real beginnings of a civil war on my hands."

Other historians think Mountbatten altered the timetable to facilitate the failure of Pakistan as a nation. M. R. Khan explains: "Some of the British leaders greeted the birth of Pakistan with the hope that partition would be a short lived affair … and [that] one day, in not too distant a future, the Indian Union would be restored." Making Pakistan "weak and vulnerable," he continues, would "ensure its early collapse." Or, as one British official put it, "Our slogan should now be 'divide in order to unite.'"

Still other historians say the decision was simply a product of Mountbatten's monumental ego. Indeed, M. R. Khan calls Mountbatten a "megalomaniac," while historian H. M. Close describes him as "extremely vain and also morally shallow." Clearly, M. R. Khan says, Mountbatten wished to "present Indian independence as his personal triumph," and didn't want anything to stand in the way of that objective. To ensure that neither he nor the British government was blamed for these disturbances, he left "little time … for trouble beforehand" and believed that "trouble afterwards would not be his responsibility, nor, he argued, would it be the responsibility of Britain."

Mountbatten likened his plan to teaching a child to ride a bicycle. "The best way to teach a youngster to cycle," he said, "is to take him to the top of a hill, put him on the seat and push him down the hill. By the time he arrives on the flat ground, he will have learnt how to cycle." (Of course, notes M. R. Khan, Mountbatten "did not consider the possibility that the youngster could have been reduced to a bundle of broken bones" by then.)

Whatever the reason behind Mountbatten's decision, it would prove disastrous.

Sir Cyril Radcliffe and the Boundary Commissions

On July 8, less than six weeks before the scheduled handover, a British barrister named Sir Cyril Radcliffe arrived in India. His mission: to decide where, exactly, the new border between Pakistan and India should lie.

In the words of journalist Frank Jacobs, Radcliffe possessed "a brilliant legal mind." What Radcliffe did *not* possess was experience setting borders; nor did any of his advisors. Moreover, Radcliffe was unfamiliar with Indian history and culture, having never visited the subcontinent before. British officials viewed Radcliffe's ignorance as an advantage, however, arguing that it would ensure his impartiality.

Sir Cyril Radcliffe led the boundary commissions charged with drawing the borders between India and Pakistan.

By the time Radcliffe arrived in India, it had already been decided that Pakistan would in fact consist of two large areas of land. One would be in the northwest, comprising the provinces of Sindh and Baluchistan in their entirety and part of Punjab. The other would cover part of Bengal to the east. Radcliffe therefore assembled two boundary commissions: one to establish the border that severed Punjab in two and the other to draw the boundary through Bengal.

Each commission consisted of four Indian judges—two selected by the Indian National Congress and two by the Muslim League—with Radcliffe as the head. Noticeably absent were members with experience drawing borders or deep knowledge of Indian geography. The makeup of these commissions—equally stocked by respected members of both parties—endowed them with, in the words of historian Lucy Chester, a "valuable veneer of justice and legitimacy" and an "appearance of political balance." However, it also resulted in a near-continual state of deadlock. On all significant issues, says historian O. H. K. Spate, the commissions "divided two and two, leaving Sir Cyril Radcliffe the invidious task of making the actual decisions."

Drawing the Lines

The job of these commissions was, according to terms that Nehru and Jinnah had agreed upon, to "demarcate the boundaries … on the basis of ascertaining the contiguous majority of areas of Muslims and non-

Muslims. In doing so, [they] will also take into account other factors." As it turned out, this task was far from straightforward. Populations of Hindus, Muslims, and other significant groups had long been intermixed, and no boundary could neatly divide them. Nor could any boundary accommodate smaller Indian groups, such as the Sikhs. As for the "other factors"—for example, economic considerations, existing administrative borders, infrastructure (such as railways and water systems), and defense requirements—Radcliffe himself observed that "differences of opinion as to [their] significance and as to the weight and value to be attached to these factors, made it impossible to arrive at any agreed line." These factors, therefore, were often set aside.

The commissions took a decidedly secretive approach to the process. That is, in the words of historian Yasmin Khan, "They retreated behind closed doors, working from maps using pen and paper, rather than walking the land and grasping for themselves the ways in which vast rivers, forests and administrative districts interlocked and could best be separated." One witness to the process, an Indian administrator named Penderel Moon, described it as it played out in Punjab: "On the floor and on a big table a number of maps of the Punjab were strewn about, variously coloured and chequered so as to show the distribution of population by communities … It became plain in a very few minutes that no one had any definite idea where we should claim that the dividing line should

THE ORIGIN OF BANGLADESH
The union between West Pakistan and East Pakistan would not last. It was not just the distance that proved problematic. The two regions had considerable linguistic, cultural, and ethnic differences. In 1971, East Pakistan broke off to become its own country, called Bangladesh.

run." Complicating matters was the fact that census information used by the commissions was out of date (and perhaps inaccurate to begin with).

Still, both commissions invited input from interested parties over the course of eight days in late July and received a large number of submissions. Given the tight timeline, however, these submissions received less attention from the commissions than perhaps they should have.

The result of these efforts was a pair of borders, collectively called the Radcliffe Line or the Radcliffe Award, that "zigzagged precariously across agricultural land, cut off communities from their sacred pilgrimage sites, paid no heed to railway lines or the integrity of forests, [and] divorced industrial plants from the agricultural hinterlands where raw materials, such as jute, were grown," Y. Khan explains. Chester notes that the Radcliffe Line "cut through the Punjab's well-developed infrastructure systems, disrupting road, telephone, and telegraph communications, but most importantly interfering with the region's vital irrigation

The border between India and Bangladesh is pictured today. After partition, the country that is now Bangladesh was a territory of Pakistan and called East Pakistan.

system." And of course, there was the inescapable fact that Pakistan itself was a nation divided, its two claims—one in the northwest and one to the east—a thousand miles apart.

The Boundary in Bengal

Drawing the Radcliffe Line through Bengal presented a number of challenges. "The province offers few, if any, satisfactory natural boundaries," Radcliffe wrote, "and its development has been on lines that do not well accord with a division by contiguous majority areas of Muslim and non-Muslim majorities." Therefore, Radcliffe proposed that the commission consider non-religious factors in drawing the border. However, he explained, "After much discussion, my colleagues found that they were unable to arrive at an agreed view on any of these major issues." Again, it was left to Radcliffe to make the final call.

Radcliffe decided on a border that divided the northern districts of Darjeeling and Jalpaiguri along the boundaries of various subdistricts, called *thanas*. The Radcliffe Line then followed the path of the Bengal-Assam Railway line until it reached the boundary between two thanas called Balurghat and Panchbib. From there, it again tracked the boundaries of various thanas until it reached the Ganges River before following a route that roughly reflected its course. At the point where the Mathabhanga River diverted from the Ganges, the Radcliffe Line went with it, following it to the boundary between the thanas of Daulatpur and Karimpur. After that, the line again tracked the boundaries of various thanas until it switched to the boundary between the districts of Khulna and 24 Parganas all the way south to the Bay of Bengal.

The Boundary in Punjab

As for the Radcliffe Line in Punjab, its northernmost point lay where the western branch of the Basantar River entered the province from the princely state of Kashmir (which, like all princely states, was allowed to decide for itself whether it would be absorbed by Pakistan or become part of India). It followed the course of the Ujh River, dividing the Gurdaspur District between Pakistan and India, before turning to traverse the Lahore district along the boundaries

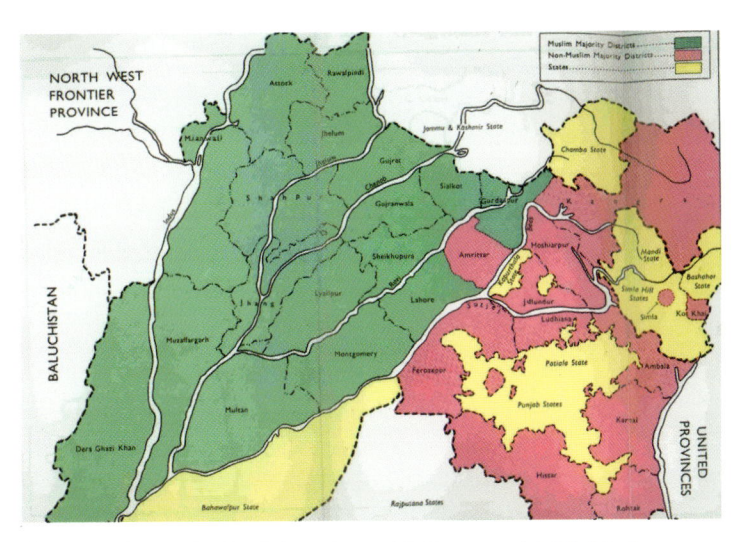

This map shows the Punjab region, with the areas highlighted according to the religious majority. Areas that had Muslim majorities are shown in green and those areas with non-Muslim majorities are shown in pink (yellow areas were princely states). The final Radcliffe Line would roughly divide these two areas, with some changes. The Gurdaspur district, for instance, was split in half.

between various subdistricts. (In Punjab, these were called *tahsils* rather than *thanas*.) When the Radcliffe Line crossed the boundary between the Lahore district and the Firozpur district, it turned to track with the Sutlej River (which also served as the boundary between the Firozpur and Montgomery districts). The line ended where it met the princely state of Bahawalpur.

The Border Revealed

Independence Day, scheduled for August 15, loomed large over Radcliffe and the members of the two border commissions. As they scrambled to finalize the

ACCESS TO ADMINISTRATIVE AND NATURAL RESOURCES

Nobody was happy with the Radcliffe Line. But the placement of the boundary generally worked in India's favor. "Pakistan was almost always given the short end of the stick, with several Muslim majority areas on the border being given to India for strategic purposes," journalist Akhilesh Pillalamarri explains. For example, the administrative machinery already in place was passed down to India, while "Pakistan would start with enormous handicaps, without an organized administration, without armed forces, without records, without equipment or military stores," Mahboobul Rahman Khan writes.

The Radcliffe Line also gave India better access to natural resources, including the fourth-largest reserve of coal in the world; to thriving cities, such as Delhi, Bombay (now Mumbai), and Calcutta; and to industrial resources, with India inheriting some 90 percent of the subcontinent's mills, factories, and other assets, leaving just 10 percent for Pakistan.

Inequalities that occurred as a result of the placement of the border were compounded by disparities in the division of physical assets belonging to the British Raj—from the most trivial (sheets of paper and library books) to the most essential (military equipment). India received 80 percent of these goods.

All these inequalities lend credence to the notion that Mountbatten compressed the handover timeline to facilitate the quick collapse of Pakistan. In this, however, he was unsuccessful.

Radcliffe Line, they kept the details secret. This caused considerable unrest and anxiety throughout India—particularly in the areas most likely to be affected.

Even when Britain did formally surrender its power over the region as scheduled, on August 15, the plans for the border remained shrouded in mystery. Although Radcliffe had finished the border on August 12, Mountbatten delayed its release until August 17, on the pretense of ensuring that the news wouldn't overshadow Independence Day celebrations. However, Chester observes, it's more likely that "Mountbatten's primary motivation was avoiding the appearance of British responsibility for the disorder that would inevitably follow the announcement." Either way, "It is difficult to see how these concerns … could outweigh the potential benefit of making administrative, military, and constabulary arrangements before the actual transfer of power took place."

For those two tense days following Independence Day, says journalist Frank Jacobs, "India and Pakistan were like conjoined twins," with the people in Punjab and Bengal "left completely in the dark about whether their homes were soon going to be in India or Pakistan."

When at last the final line was revealed, the overwhelming response was one of shock and unhappiness. Simply put, no one on either side was satisfied. Jinnah called the border "an unjust, incomprehensible and even perverse award," and described the geography of the new nation of Pakistan

Lord Louis Mountbatten (*top, standing*) formally declares India's independence on August 15, 1947.

as "maimed, mutilated and moth-eaten." The matter, however, was settled. Prior to the release of the border, Mountbatten had, in his words, "taken assurances from the representatives of India and Pakistan that they would accept the Award of the Commission whatever it might be."

Even Radcliffe conceded that the line was far from perfect. "I am conscious," he wrote, "that there are legitimate criticisms to be made of it, as there are, I think, of any other line that might be chosen ... I am conscious, too, that the Award cannot go far towards satisfying sentiments and aspirations deeply held on either side." This may explain why Radcliffe refused his fee of 40,000 rupees (about $6,956 in today's dollars), burned his papers, and, on Independence Day, departed India for England, never to return.

In Radcliffe's defense, the compressed time frame, dictated by Mountbatten, made it impossible to properly analyze the myriad factors involved in drawing an international border. Indeed, years later, Radcliffe would tell journalist Kuldeep Nayar that "I had no alternative; the time at my disposal was so short that I could not do a better job. Given the same period, I would do the same thing. However, if I had two to three years, I might have improved on what I did."

While "Radcliffe's line was far from perfect," Chester observes, "it is important to note that alternative borders would not necessarily have provided a significant improvement." Jacobs agrees: "His border may have been hastily and arbitrarily drawn, but it is hard to see how any new, religion-based border across relatively integrated lands would not have led to chaos, violence and bloodshed."

CHAPTER FIVE

The Fallout

Even before Mountbatten released the Radcliffe Line, tensions had mounted between Muslims, Hindus, and Sikhs, particularly in areas where the border was likely to fall. Sporadic violence peppered both sides of the line. Once the border was set, those tensions intensified, leading to many months of violence and millions of displaced people.

On the "Wrong Side" of the Border

After partition, Muslims in India and Hindus and Sikhs in Pakistan found themselves "marooned"—that is, on the "wrong side" of the new border. As a result, notes historian Yasmin Khan, "The predominant feeling was one of intense confusion, angst and anxiety about the future from all sections of society." As one Hindu

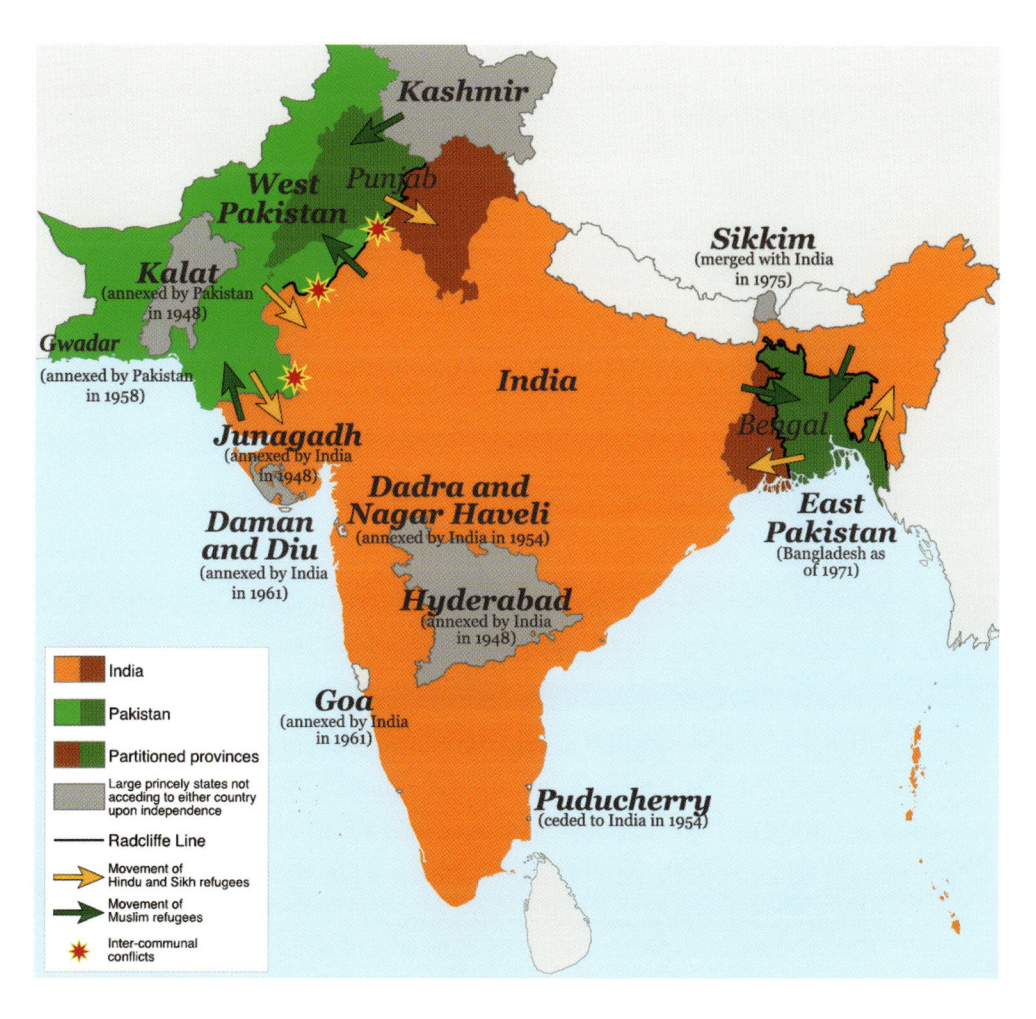

Millions of refugees were displaced by partition.

stranded in Pakistan said, "I cannot reconcile myself to the very conception of a divided India in which I become an alien in a great part of my own beloved motherland, and a citizen of a new Muslim theocratic state created overnight."

The Fallout 81

Those on the "wrong side"—and there were many—weren't only concerned about living as "aliens" or minorities. They also feared they would be oppressed and exploited, forced to convert, or even killed. This fear sparked widespread violence and mass migration.

Widespread Violence

The horrific violence wrought by partition was carried out by two groups: those on the "wrong side" of the boundary, who, according to Y. Khan, fought to "purify and cleanse their home areas, to reverse the line or to rob it of its meaning"; and those on the "right side" of the border, who sought to solidify their power by purging their lands of the "other"—that is, anyone who was not like them. For Hindus and Muslims alike, their religious identity had taken precedence over all other considerations. As a result, both these populations engaged in (and suffered from) the violence in equal measures.

For many, the violence was almost unimaginably brutal. Historians Ian Talbot and Gurharpal Singh write, "There are numerous eyewitness accounts of the maiming and mutilation of victims." Pregnant women and babies were among those who suffered the worst of these atrocities. Y. Khan records some horrific scenes: "A whole village might be hacked alive, or shot against walls by impromptu firing squads using machine guns." She also notes that "gangs deliberately derailed trains,

Indian soldiers sift through the debris of a building destroyed during the violent aftermath of partition.

massacring their passengers one by one or setting the carriages ablaze with petrol."

"This was not," says Y. Khan, "haphazard frantic killing but, at its worst, routine, timetabled and systematic ethnic cleansing." It seemed, however, that the aim of the perpetrators was not just to kill people, but to break them. Hence, "ritual humiliation and conversions from one faith to another occurred, alongside systematic looting and robbery clearly carried out with the intention of ruining lives."

Women were routinely attacked and brutally mistreated during this post-partition violence, sometimes abducted and kept "as permanent hostages, captives or forced wives." Still others were forced into prostitution. Many women and girls who escaped these miserable fates found themselves rejected by their families because, says Y. Khan, "their 'character' was now spoilt." Often, these women committed suicide—either voluntarily or because their families forced them to. Some were even murdered by their own relatives in so-called honor killings.

Leaders in both Pakistan and India pleaded for order, to no avail. Perhaps in an attempt to protect the "other" in Pakistan, Jinnah even called for religious freedom in the Muslim homeland, saying, "You may belong to any religion or caste or creed—that has nothing to do with the business of the State." Sadly, this call for freedom fell on deaf ears.

These leaders did not, however, deploy the military. Simply put, they couldn't. Just as partition called for the split of India's land in two, it demanded the division of its military—and the culling of Muslim soldiers from the existing British Indian Army to form the new Pakistani Armed Forces was not yet complete. There were British troops in the region that could have been used to restore order, but Mountbatten forbade this. He believed the British were no longer duty-bound to protect their former subjects on the subcontinent—and so they didn't.

As for outside help, little came. Bruised and battered by World War II, Europe turned inward. And although the United States favored Indian independence, it stayed out of the conflict. Finally, as for international charities like the International Red Cross, the partition crisis was simply too widespread for them to address it effectively.

Fortunately, many Hindus and Muslims performed lifesaving acts of mercy and charity. "Some individuals saved the lives of neighbors, friends and strangers of different communities, even by risking their own lives," Y. Khan writes. "Others gave word of impending attacks to their neighbors, sheltered large numbers of people, smuggled food to the stranded and helped secretly move them from danger in the dead of night by lending transport or arranging disguises or armed protection."

Mass Migration

During the summer of 1947, in the run-up to partition, a trickle of refugees across the border areas in either direction had begun. Some people migrated

PARTITION-RELATED DEATHS

No one knows exactly how many people died because of partition (whether by violence, disease, starvation, or exhaustion), but estimates vary between several hundred thousand to two million deaths.

Refugees swarm trains in an attempt to escape sectarian violence.

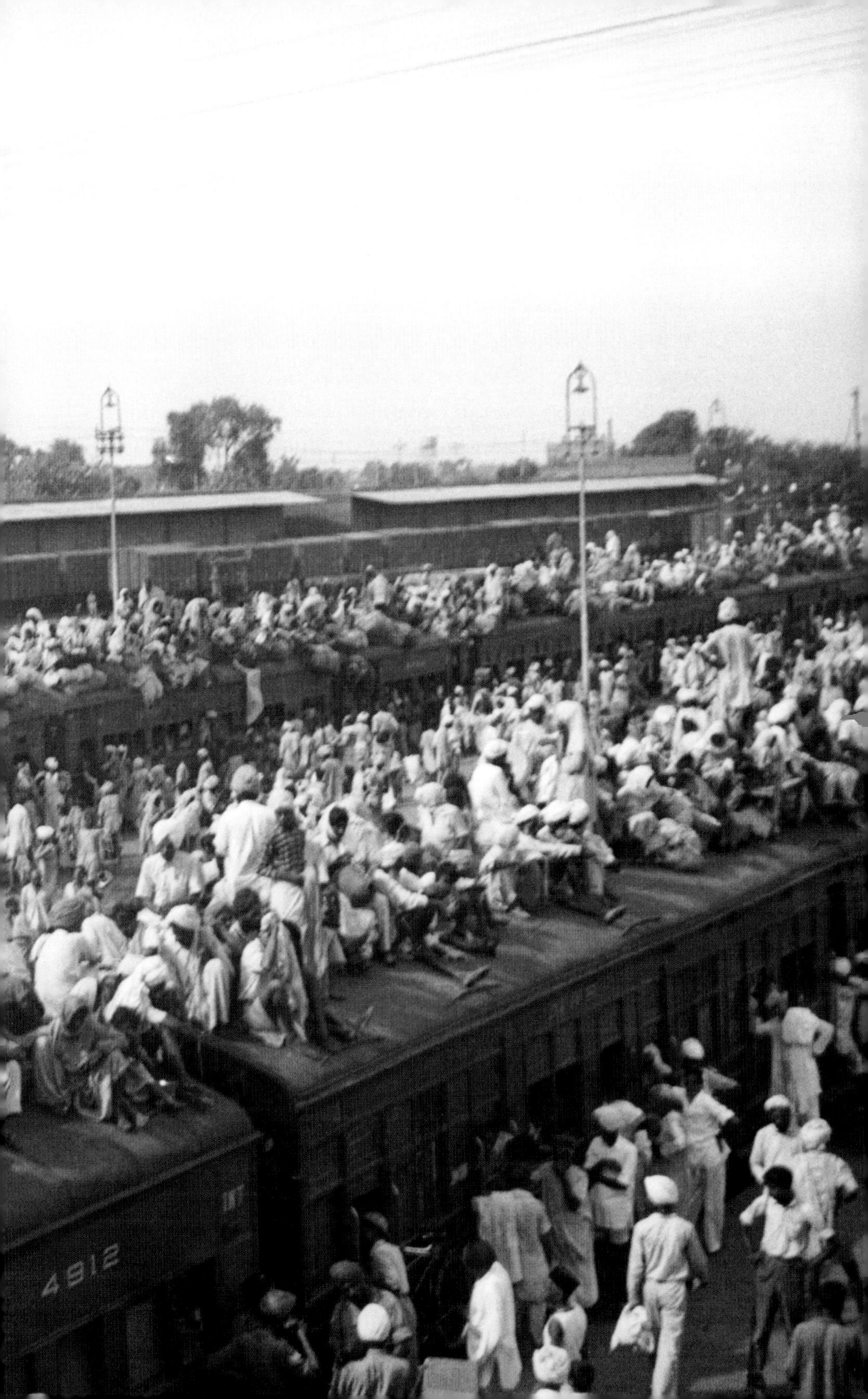
4912

because they were already facing violence as tensions between Muslims and Hindus escalated; others because they simply anticipated that violence. Still, their numbers were relatively small—perhaps one hundred thousand in all. Following partition, however, "Muslim communities were drummed out of India, just as Hindus and Sikhs were hounded out of many parts of Pakistan," says Y. Khan. By November 1947, eight million refugees had crossed the Radcliffe Line in both directions. By the end of 1948, that number had swelled to twelve million.

Some refugees traveled by plane, others by car or truck, others by ox and cart, and still others by train. However, the vast majority of these refugees walked. "Foot caravans of destitute refugees fleeing the violence stretched for 50 miles [80 km] and more," writes Indian American foreign affairs analyst Nisid Hajari. The trip, he says, was dangerous: "As the peasants trudged along wearily, mounted guerrillas burst out of the tall crops that lined the road and culled them like sheep." Those refugees who traveled by train were likewise targeted: "Special refugee trains, filled to bursting when they set out, suffered repeated ambushes along the way. All too often they crossed the border in funereal silence, blood seeping from under their carriage doors."

The weakest refugees—those who were too old, sick, exhausted, or hungry to complete the journey—wound up in hastily assembled "camps" (hardly an appropriate term for these places, because, in the words of future Indian president Dr. Zakir Hussain, they were

Many refugees were forced to escape by foot, bringing with them only what they could carry.

CONFLICT OVER KASHMIR

Since partition, India and Pakistan have faced off in multiple wars over a region called Kashmir. Kashmir is situated to the north of India and Pakistan and shares a border with both, although its border with Pakistan is significantly longer.

Kashmir has a long history. Settlement of the region dates to 3000 BCE. Early Kashmiris lived simply, subsisting primarily by hunting and fishing but also by cultivating crops like wheat, barley, and lentils.

In ancient times, Kashmir fell first to one, then another of a series of rulers. (These included one woman, Queen Didda, who ruled during the second half of the tenth century CE.) Most of these rulers were either Buddhist or Hindu—and so were most Kashmiris. That changed in 1339 CE, when a man named Shah Mir became the first Muslim ruler of Kashmir. This marked the beginning of nearly five hundred years of Muslim rule over the region and a shift toward Islam among the Kashmiri population as a whole.

In 1819, Kashmir fell to the Sikhs. To solidify their power, the Sikhs enacted several anti-Muslim laws, including one that banned the Muslim call to prayer. Fortunately for Kashmiris, who by then were overwhelmingly Muslim, Sikh rule was relatively short. It ended in 1846, when the East India Company defeated the Sikhs in the First Anglo-Sikh War. The British victors folded Kashmir into a larger state, called the Princely State of Kashmir and Jammu, and placed it under Hindu rule, despite its population being overwhelmingly Muslim. These minority Hindu rulers heavily oppressed the Muslim majority, subjecting them to discriminatory laws, high taxes, and even slavery.

In 1947, British officials demanded that the rulers of all princely states join either India or Pakistan following partition. They were to make this decision taking into account their geographical proximity to these countries and the wishes of their people. But Maharaja Hari Singh, the ruler of Kashmir, preferred to remain independent.

Kashmir remains a disputed territory. It borders both Pakistan and India. Today, India, Pakistan, and China all administer parts of the region.

In late 1947, a Muslim uprising, supported by Pakistan, forced the Maharaja to turn to India for help extinguishing the revolt. India agreed—provided the Maharaja accede to India. He agreed, marking the launch of the First Indo-Pakistani War. India emerged victorious, and Kashmir was turned over to India.

India considered the accession to be provisional. That is, it would stand until officials could conduct a plebiscite to determine the will of the Kashmiri people. For various reasons, this plebiscite never occurred, causing relations between India and Pakistan to sour even further.

Although Pakistan has since reclaimed a portion of Kashmir, the conflict over the region continues even today, making it one of the longest-running territorial disputes in the world.

The Fallout

"areas in which humanity was dumped"). Conditions were appalling, mainly due to overcrowding. At one camp, as many as twenty-five thousand people arrived each day. The poor sanitation in these camps resulted in widespread disease and death.

This mass migration took officials by surprise. When asked by a reporter in June 1947 if he foresaw a mass transfer of population, Mountbatten had replied, "Personally I don't see it. There are many physical and practical difficulties involved." Therefore, the final partition plan made no allowances for a mass population exchange, assuming that many Hindus and Sikhs would remain in Pakistan, and that many Muslims would remain in India. Indeed, it was believed that those minorities who remained behind would act as guarantors against the persecution of minorities on the other side. Sadly, this was not the case.

An End to the Upheaval

At the height of the upheaval after partition, "there was a feeling," says Y. Khan, "that the new states might be on the brink of falling, irretrievably, into an abyss." By the end of 1948, however, the upheaval had largely abated. Still, it left a lasting mark, permanently changing the population distribution in both India and Pakistan. As journalist William Dalrymple explains, "In 1941, Karachi, designated the first capital of Pakistan, was 47.6 per cent Hindu. Delhi, the capital of independent India, was one-third Muslim. By the end of the decade, almost all the Hindus of Karachi had fled, while two hundred thousand Muslims had been forced out of Delhi." Seventy years later, these changes have endured.

An end to the upheaval stabilized the region, freeing both India and Pakistan to repair their broken societies and economies. "In both countries, the state paid for the construction of schools, dispensaries, houses and workshops," notes Y. Khan. "The government created job centers, employed refugees in public works, cleared land in forested areas to make space for displaced accommodation, built training centers to teach women skills such as soap-making and embroidery, and retrained men as mechanics, carpenters, spinners, paper-makers, shoemakers and printers."

Within just a few years, "visitors were surprised by the speed of change and the ways in which these events had faded from view," says Y. Khan. Still, she adds, "Partition left deep and ragged fault lines" and "had a widespread psychological impact."

Hardened Borders

At the advent of partition, both Indians and Pakistanis assumed the borders between the two countries would be soft, allowing for easy travel between the two. That was not the case. Instead, says Y. Khan, the two countries were "hermetically sealed off from each other," meaning that people who had moved from one to the other could never return. This separation, enforced by tight restrictions on border crossing, "was the most long-lasting and divisive aspect of Partition," Y. Khan concludes.

With these hardened borders came more rigid national identities. Stating allegiance to one country or the other became mandatory. It wasn't enough for citizens to declare themselves *in favor of* India or Pakistan, however; they also had to declare themselves *against* the other. Ultimately, says Y. Khan, "Indian and Pakistani ideas of nationhood were carved out diametrically, in definition against each other." As a result, people in both nations soon saw each other as enemies.

Continuing Conflict

The mass upheaval following partition may have ended in late 1948, but the conflict between the two countries has continued. Since partition, India and Pakistan have fought multiple wars against each other, spending vast sums on weapons and even developing nuclear arsenals along the way. In 1999, the two countries narrowly avoided nuclear war. "Both governments," says Y. Khan, "[have] escalated their real militarization in response to the perceived aggression of the other."

It is not simply that the two nations are at loggerheads. Their citizens are, too—in part because interaction between Indian and Pakistani citizens is limited. "Pakistani bitterness against India and Indians and Indian bitterness against Pakistan and Pakistani[s] are facts of life in South Asia," writes scholar Lucy

Chester. Those Indians and Pakistani who do long for peace are stymied by "government propaganda and certain streams of public discourse, including those generated by media and educational institutions" that "reinforce cross-border resentments." Today, notes Dalrymple, "both India and Pakistan remain crippled by the narratives built around the memories of the crimes of partition, as politicians (particularly in India) and the military (particularly in Pakistan) continue to stoke the hatreds of 1947 for their own ends."

Not surprisingly, Indians and Pakistanis also view partition through completely different lenses. Many Indians see partition as a direct result of the Muslim League's refusal to work toward a unified India, failing to account for their own role in those discussions. In contrast, Pakistanis have reframed partition as a war of liberation—a story of "martyrdom, courage and victimhood." Of course, neither version is entirely correct.

Hope for the Future

"It is well past time," says writer and foreign affairs analyst Nisid Hajari, "that the heirs to Nehru and Jinnah finally put 1947's furies to rest." Unfortunately, for now, the rivalry between India and Pakistan "is getting more, rather than less, dangerous," because of growing nuclear arsenals, the proliferation of militant groups, increasing religious extremism, and the policies of hard-line governments on both sides.

A flag-lowering ceremony is played out at the Wagah border between India and Pakistan.

Despite all these factors, says Y. Khan, "a paradoxical fascination with and attraction to the former homeland lingers" on both sides of the Radcliffe Line. And on both sides, a great many people hope that this fascination and attraction—the product of millennia of shared history—will one day translate to a lasting peace between these two nations.

CHRONOLOGY

- **60,000 BCE** Early humans settle the Indus Valley.

- **3300 BCE** The Indus Valley Civilization forms.

- **960 CE** Muslim invaders begin attacking Hindu and Buddhist kingdoms in northern India.

- **1173** Sultan Mu'izz ad-Din Muhammad Ghori successfully occupies northern India.

- **1206** The Delhi sultanate takes control of India and will reign until 1526.

- **1526** The Mughal Empire conquers the Delhi sultanate.

- **1758** The East India Company establishes company rule in India.

- **1857** The Indian Rebellion of 1857 begins on May 10.

- **1858** Britain passes the Government of India Act 1858. It liquidates the East India Company and places India under the rule of the British government.

CHRONOLOGY

- **1885**   A group of Indians forms the Indian National Congress on December 28.

- **1892**   Britain passes the Indian Councils Act of 1892, the first of several bills granting Indians greater autonomy. Others include the Morley-Minto Reforms (1909), the Montagu-Chelmsford Reforms (1919), and the Government of India Act 1935.

- **1905**   To "divide and conquer," British officials split the province of Bengal in two on July 7.

- **1906**   A group of Muslims forms the All India Muslim League on December 30.

- **1916**   The Indian National Congress and the Muslim League sign the Lucknow Pact in December to pressure the British government for greater autonomy.

- **1919**   British soldiers fire on thousands of peaceful protesters in Amritsar on April 13 in what became known as the Amritsar Massacre (also known as the Jallianwala Bagh Massacre).

- **1920**   Gandhi launches the noncooperation movement on August 1.

- **1940** The Muslim League adopts the Lahore Resolution, which calls for the formation of Pakistan.

- **1942** In March, members of the Cripps Mission offer India independence after World War II in exchange for the continued support of its leaders in the war effort, but talks break down.

- **1942** Gandhi launches the Quit India movement on August 8. The British crush the movement and imprison tens of thousands of Congress officials.

- **1945** King George announces on August 15 that Britain will grant India's independence.

- **1946** Indian elections act as a de facto referendum on the formation of Pakistan. The "referendum" passes.

- **1946** In May, members of the Cabinet Mission attempt to broker a compromise between the Congress and the Muslim League. However, talks break down.

CHRONOLOGY

- **1946**   Direct Action Day on August 16, a Muslim League holiday, devolves into a three-day clash between Muslims and Hindus in which thousands die.

- **1947**   On February 20, British prime minister Clement Attlee announces a June 1948 handover deadline. Lord Louis Mountbatten moves up the deadline by almost a year. August 15 is Indian Independence Day. (Pakistan's Independence Day is celebrated on August 14.) Mountbatten releases final plans for the Radcliffe Line on August 17, sparking widespread violence and mass migration.

- **1948**   The violence and migration sparked by partition winds down around December.

GLOSSARY

barrister A lawyer.

bicameral Describes a legislative body comprised of two branches.

caste A hereditary social class.

census An official count of a population (such as that of a country).

clemency Mercy or lenience.

commonwealth A loose federation of nations, specifically, nations formerly part of the British Empire.

communal Of or relating to a community; of, relating to, or based on racial or cultural groups.

constabulary Relating to law enforcement.

dominion A nation with sovereign status.

dynasty A powerful group or family that maintains its position, especially as the ruler of a country, kingdom, or state, for a considerable time.

mahatma A title given to a person regarded with reverence or loving respect.

manifesto The public declaration of policies and aims issued by a political party or other group.

megalomaniac Describes a person obsessed with his or her own power.

GLOSSARY

paradoxical Describes something that seems self-contradictory or even absurd.

pilau Another term for pilaf, an Indian or Middle Eastern rice dish.

plebiscite A direct vote by the people on a particular issue.

satyagraha A policy of nonviolent political protest or resistance.

sectarian Related to different sects or religions.

secularist Someone who believes in the separation of church and state.

sedition The act of rebelling or inciting rebellion against the state.

sovereignty The authority of a state to govern itself.

subcontinent A large part of a continent.

sultanate Similar to a kingdom, but ruled by a sultan, the sovereign especially of a Muslim state.

swaraj Self-governance.

viceroy One who governs a colony on behalf of a sovereign.

vivisection The act of cutting into a live body.

FURTHER INFORMATION

Books

Butalia, Urvashi. *Partition: The Long Shadow*. New Delhi, India: Zubaan/Penguin, 2015.

Hajari, Nisid. *Midnight's Furies: The Deadly Legacy of India's Partition*. Stroud, UK: Amberley Publishing, 2015.

Khan, Yasmin. *The Great Partition: The Making of India and Pakistan, New Edition*. New Haven, CT: Yale University Press, 2017.

Sarna, Mohinder Singh. *Savage Harvest: Stories of Partition*. New Delhi, India: Rupa Publications, 2013.

Wolpert, Stanley. *Shameful Flight*. Oxford, UK: Oxford University Press, 2009.

Websites

Borders and Bloodshed: The Making of India and Pakistan
www.cnn.com/2017/08/08/asia/gallery/india-pakistan-independence-photos/index.html

A series of photos illustrates key moments in the process of partition.

India-Pakistan Relations: A 50-Year History
asiasociety.org/education/india-pakistan-relations-50-year-history

Beginning in 1947, the Asia Society Center for Global Education offers a historical overview of the relationship between India and Pakistan, including key statistics and insight into both countries' nuclear testing.

FURTHER INFORMATION

Timeline: India/Pakistan Relations
www.aljazeera.com/indepth/spotlight/kashmirthe forgottenconflict/2011/06/2011615113058224115.html

A comprehensive timeline outlines India-Pakistan relations, from 1947 to present day.

Videos

"Michael Palin at the India-Pakistan Border Ceremony"
www.youtube.com/watch?v=n9y2qtaopbE

The BBC visits an annual ceremony acted out at the India-Pakistan border.

"Partition: Borders of Blood"
www.aljazeera.com/programmes/101east/2017/08/partition-borders-blood-170809102605065.html

A two-part video special examines the long history of tensions between India and Pakistan.

"Three Muslim Women Reflect on the Partition of British India"
www.bbc.com/news/av/uk-england-leeds-40936148/three-muslim-women-reflect-on-partition-of-british-india

A woman who lost two hundred family members during post-partition violence recalls the horrific atrocities committed at that time, sharing these stories with her family.

BIBLIOGRAPHY

Ahmed, Khaled. "The Secular Mussulman." *Friday Times* (Lahore), May 23, 1998.

Anjum, Zafar. *Iqbal: The Life of a Poet, Philosopher and Politician.* Gurgaon, India: Random House India, 2014.

Berriedale Keith, Arthur, ed. "Lucknow Pact Between Congress and Muslim League 1916." In *Speeches and Documents on Indian Policy, 1750–1921, Vol. II.* London, UK: Humphrey Milford, Oxford University Press, 1922. http://www.indiaofthepast.org/contribute-memories/read-contributions/major-events-pre-1950/319-lucknow-pact-between-congress-and-muslim-league1916.

Brown, Judith M. *Gandhi's Rise to Power: Indian Politics 1915–1922.* Cambridge, UK: Cambridge University Press, 1974.

Chester, Lucy. "The 1947 Partition: Drawing the Indo-Pakistani Boundary." *American Diplomacy*, February 15, 2002. http://www.unc.edu/depts/diplomat/archives_roll/2002_01-03/chester_partition/chester_partition.html.

Chhabra, G. S. *Advanced Study in the History of Modern India (Volume 3: 1920–1947).* New Delhi, India: Lotus Press, 2005.

Dabas, Maninder. "Here's How the Radcliffe Line Was Drawn on This Day and Lahore Could Not Become a Part of India." *Indiatimes*, August 17, 2017. https://www.indiatimes.com/news/india/here-s-how-radcliff-line-was-drawn-on-this-day-and-lahore-could-not-become-a-part-of-india-328012.html.

Dalrymple, William. "The Great Divide: The Violent Legacy of Indian Partition." *New Yorker*, June 29, 2015. https://www.newyorker.com/magazine/2015/06/29/the-great-divide-books-dalrymple.

Hajari, Nisid. *Midnight's Furies: The Deadly Legacy of India's Partition.* Stroud, UK: Amberley Publishing, 2015.

BIBLIOGRAPHY

Jacobs, Frank. "Peacocks at Sunset." *New York Times*, July 3, 2012. https://opinionator.blogs.nytimes.com/2012/07/03/peacocks-at-sunset.

Jinnah, Muhammad Ali. "Presidential Address by Muhammad Ali Jinnah to the Muslim League." Columbia University. Accessed October 24, 2017. http://www.columbia.edu/itc/mealac/pritchett/00islamlinks/txt_jinnah_lahore_1940.html.

Khan, Mahboobul Rhaman. "Mountbatten and the 'Hurried Scuttle.'" *Pakistan Journal of History and Culture* 19, no. 1 (1998): 17–25.

Khan, Yasmin. *The Great Partition: The Making of India and Pakistan, New Edition*. New Haven, CT: Yale University Press, 2017.

Maddison, Angus. *Class Structure and Economic Growth: India and Pakistan Since the Moghuls*. Milton Park, UK: Taylor & Francis, 1971.

Menon, V. P. *Transfer of Power in India*. Princeton, NJ: Princeton University Press, 1957.

Metcalf, Thomas. *Ideologies of the Raj*. Cambridge, UK: Cambridge University Press, 1995.

Mohiuddin, Yasmeen Niaz. *Pakistan: A Global Studies Handbook*. Santa Barbara, CA: ABC-CLIO, 2007.

Moore, R. J. "Mountbatten, India and the Commonwealth." *Journal of Commonwealth and Comparative Politics* 19, no. 1 (1981): 5–43.

Murthy, Srinivas. *Mahatma Gandhi and Leo Tolstoy Letters*. Long Beach, CA: Long Beach Publications, 1987.

Pati, Budheswar. *India and the First World War*. New Delhi, India: Atlantic Publishers and Distributors Pvt Ltd., 1996.

Roberts, Andrew. *Eminent Churchillians*. London, UK: Weidenfeld & Nicolson, 1995.

Sheikh, Zubair. "Analyzing the Text: The Lahore (Pakistan) Resolution." Let Us Build Pakistan, March 23, 2011. https://lubpak.com/archives/43698.

Singh, Jaswant. *Jinnah: India–Partition–Independence.* Oxford, UK: Oxford University Press, 2009.

Spate, O. H. K. "The Partition of the Punjab and Bengal." *Geographical Journal* 110, no. 4 (1947): 201–218.

Subramanian, Samanth. "The Long View: The Partition Before Partition." *New York Times*, October 30, 2011. https://india.blogs.nytimes.com/2011/10/03/the-long-view-the-partition-before-partition.

Talbot, Ian. "Jinnah and the Making of Pakistan." *History Today* 34, no. 2 (1984).

Talbot, Ian, and Gurharpal Singh. *The Partition of India.* Cambridge, UK: Cambridge University Press, 2009.

Tellis, Ashley J. "Are India-Pakistan Peace Talks Worth a Damn?" Washington, DC: Carnegie Endowment for International Peace, 2017. http://carnegieendowment.org/files/India-Pakistan_Peace_Talks_final1.pdf.

Tharoor, Shashi. "The Partition: The British Game of 'Divide and Rule.'" Al Jazeera, August 10, 2017. http://www.aljazeera.com/indepth/opinion/2017/08/partition-british-game-divide-rule-170808101655163.html.

———. "Why the Indian Soldiers of WW1 [sic] Were Forgotten." *BBC News*, July 2, 2015. http://www.bbc.com/news/magazine-33317368.

Tilak, Bal Gangadhar. *Bal Gangadhar Talik: His Writings and Speeches.* Madras, India: Ganesh & Co., 1919.

Tunzelmann, Alex von. *Indian Summer: The Secret History of the End of an Empire.* New York: Picador, 2008.

United Nations. "Reports of International Arbitral Awards: Boundary Disputes Between India and Pakistan Relating to

BIBLIOGRAPHY

the Interpretation of the Report of the Bengal Boundary Commission." United Nations, January 26, 1950. http://legal.un.org/riaa/cases/vol_XXI/1-51.pdf.

Victoria, Queen. "Queen Victoria's Proclamation of 1858," in *Indian Constitutional Documents*, by Panchanandas Mukherji, 359. Calcutta, India: Thacker Spink & Co, 1915.

Wheeler, Mortimer. *The Cambridge History of India*. Cambridge, UK: Cambridge University Press, 1960.

Wolpert, Stanley. *Gandhi's Passion*. Oxford, UK: Oxford University Press, 2002.

———. *Jinnah of Pakistan*. Oxford, UK: Oxford University Press, 2015.

———. *Shameful Flight*. Oxford, UK: Oxford University Press, 2009.

Zehra, Sumbul. "The Lucknow Pact." *Lucknow (India) Observer*, December 5, 2015. http://lucknowobserver.com/the-lucknow-pact.

INDEX

Page numbers in **boldface** are illustrations.

Amritsar, **9**
   Amritsar Massacre, 32–35
Attlee, Clement, **51**, 52–53, 59, 61

Babur, 14, **15**
Bangladesh (East Pakistan), 62–63, **63**, 72, **73**,
barrister, 68
Bengal, 53, 56–57, 70, 73, 77
   partition of, 22, 24–25
bicameral, 42
Bombay (Mumbai), 40, **48**, **64**, 76
British Indian Army, 7, 26–29, 46, 84
British Raj, 4–7, 12–13, 17–34, 38–39, 42–43, 45–47, 49–52, 76
   Indian independence and partition, 50–61, 65, 67–79, 80–92
   map of empire, **6**
   Parliament and, 17, 42, 50
Buddhism, 14, 22, 39, 90

Cabinet Mission, 54–55
Calcutta, 22, 55–57, **56**, 76
castes, 34, 42–43, 84
census, 39, 72
Christians, 22, 39

clemency, 13
Commonwealth, British, 29
communal, 58
constabulary, 77
Cripps, Richard Stafford, 47
Cripps Mission, 47–48
Curzon, Lord George, **21**, 22, 24–25

Delhi, 13–14, 52, 76, 92–93
Delhi sultanate, 12, 14–15
Direct Action Day, 55–57
"divide and rule," 22–24
dominion status, 29, 47
dynasties, 14

East India Company, 12–13, 23, 90

flag-lowering ceremony, **96**

Gandhi, Mohandas K., **33**, 34–35, **41**, 44–45, 47–49, 58, 61
   as mahatma, 35
George V, King 29
George VI, King, 50–52, **51**
Government of India Act 1919, 31, 42
Government of India Act 1935, 42–43

Index **109**

INDEX

Hindus/Hinduism, 6–7, 12, 14, 20, 22–25, 34–35, 36–39, 43–44, 49–50, 52–53, 57–58, 67, 71, 90
during and after partition, 80–88, 92–94

Independence Day, **64**, **66**, 75, 77, 79
India
independence, 6, 8, 60–61, 65, 67, 75–77
maps, **5**, **62**, **63**
road toward independence, 10–35, 36, 42–43, 47–55, 59
Indian Army, 7, 26, 84
Indian National Congress, **19**, 20, 26, 29–30, 32, 36–40, 42–44, 45, 47, 49, 52–55, 57–58, 61, 70
Indian subcontinent
early history, 10–12
maps, **5**, **62**, **63**
Indus Valley Civilization, 10–12, **11**
Iqbal, Muhammad, **37**, 38

Jinnah, Muhammad Ali, 40–41, **41**, 43, 47, 53–55, 59–61, **60**, 70, 77, 84, 95

Karachi, 92–93

Kashmir, **5**, 74, 90–91, **91**

Lahore Resolution, 44
Lucknow Pact, 29–30

manifesto, 43
megalomaniac, 67
Minto, Earl of, 25
Montagu, Edwin, 30–31
Montagu-Chelmsford Reforms, 31
Mountbatten, Lord Louis, 59–61, **60**, 65–68, 76–79, **78**, 80, 84, 92
Mountbatten Plan, 60–61, 65
Mughal Empire, 12
Mu'izz ad-Din Muhammad Ghori, 14
Muslim League, 25–26, **26–27**, 29–30, 36, 38–40, 42–43, 47, 50, 53–57, 60–61, 70
Muslims/Islam, 7, 12, 14, 20, 22–26, 35, 36–42, 43–44, 49–50, 52–54, 56–58, 67, 70–71, 73, 90–91, 95
during and after partition, 80–88, 92–94

natural resources, 4, 22, 76
Nehru, Jawaharlal, 44, 52, 58, **60**, 61, 70, 95

110   The Partition of India

Pakistan
  call for creation of, 36–45, 50, 53–55, 60–61
  creation of, 6, 10, 26, 40–41, 60, 62–63, 65–79, 80, 95
  maps, **5**, **63**
Pakistani Armed Forces, 7, 84
paradoxical, 96
partition
  agreement on, 58–60
  announcement of, 65–68
  call for by Muslims, 36–45, 50, 53–55, 60
  deaths as result of, 7–8, 57, 82–83, 85, 88
  drawing the border, 68–75
  lasting effects of, 8–9, 92–96
  migration due to, 8, 80, **81**, 82, 85–92
  opposition to, 39, 44–45, 54, 61, 67, 76
  takes effect, 77–79, 80–93
  violence and, 7–8, **9**, 57, 79, 80, 82–84, **83**, 88
pilau, 7
plebiscite, 91
princely states, 17, 74, 90
Punjab, 53, 70–75, **75**, 77

Quit India movement, **48**, 48–50, 52

Radcliffe, Cyril, 68–71, **69**, 73–75, 77, 79
Radcliffe Line, 72–79, **75**, 80, 88, 96
refugees, **81**, 85–88, **86–87**, **89**, 92–93
riots, **56**, 57–58
Rowlatt Act, 31–32

satyagraha, 34
sectarian violence, 7–8, **9**, 57, 79, 80, 82–84, **83**, 88
secularist, 40
sedition, 31
Sikhs, 22–23, 36, 39, 71, 80, 88, 90, 92
Sindh, 38, 53, 70
sovereignty, 29, 44
Suhrawardy, Husseyn, 56
swaraj, 34–35

viceroy, 17, 22, 25, 31, 49, 59
Victoria, Queen, 13, **16**
vivisection, 61

World War I, 26–29, **28**, 30–31, 46
World War II, 6, **45**, 45–47, **46**, 49–50, 52–53, 85

ABOUT THE AUTHOR

Kate Shoup has written more than forty books and has edited hundreds more. When not working, Shoup loves to travel, watch IndyCar racing, ski, read, and ride her motorcycle. She lives in Indianapolis with her husband, her daughter, and their dog.